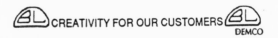

RELATIONSHIP DYNAMICS

Theory and Analysis

JAMES MUSGRAVE
MICHAEL ANNISS

THE FREE PRESS

New York   London   Toronto   Sydney   Singapore

THE FREE PRESS
A Division of Simon & Schuster Inc.
1230 Avenue of the Americas
New York, NY 10020

THE FREE PRESS and colophon are trademarks
of Simon & Schuster Inc.

Manufactured in the United States of America

10   9   8   7   6   5   4   3   2   1

Library of Congress Cataloging-in-Publication Data

Musgrave, James, 1951–
    Relationship dynamics: theory and analysis / James Musgrave,
    Michael Anniss.
        p.   cm.
    Includes bibliographical references (p.   ) and index.
    ISBN 0–684–82449–3
    1. Communication in organizations.   2. Interpersonal relations.
3. Line and staff organization.   4. Customer relations.
I. Anniss, Michael, 1958–   .
II. Title.
HD30.3.M88   1996
658.4'5—dc20   96–10516
                                                         CIP

This book is dedicated to my sons—Alastair, Neddy, Christopher, Joseph, and Donald—and to my wife, Heather; her passionate belief in me has carried me further than ever possible on my own, thanks.

—James Musgrave

This book is dedicated to my family—Jane, Stephen, and Kirsty—and to my niece Katie, whose recent death has snuffed out one of the bright lights in this world.

—Michael Anniss

CONTENTS

PREFACE

Relationship Dynamics is offered to its readers as something more than a management theory, one that has an analytical framework of process and application. It is a tool set and prism through which the amorphous and aggregated processes of life become visible, clearer, and more understandable. We have fashioned its format, methodology, and content so that a variety of management and socioeconomic concerns, the most important of those being the ability to observe and understand, are addressed.

A word of advice: there is no panacea, there is no quick fix, there is no prescriptive formula that will whisk our problems away. In fact, if there is one goal for *Relationship Dynamics*, it is to enable its reader to better comprehend his framework of association by developing the skill to better understand the connectedness, scope of operation, roles and "relationship" drivers, of the entities within the framework. Management executives, of all grades, derive confidence and are better able to make appropriate responses when they know

- how and why things work the way they do
- where things could go, depending on who and what is driving things
- what the current bounds of association seek and will tolerate
- why and how these current bounds may have to change as well as the type and extent of the "inertia" that the present setup has vis-à-vis any subsequent change requirements.

Relationship Dynamics will benefit those who are looking for real understanding. Also, it is important to be aware that many popular management approaches and "solutions" are mechanistic and deterministic, taking little, if any, cognizance of the actual realities and limitations under which all approaches and solutions must be applied. That orientation has led, particularly in the United States and Britain, to the development of a management culture that constantly pursues the quick fix. Our managers labor under a preoccupation to do rather than to think. Indeed, often action is mistaken for achievement, while data collection and analysis pass for understanding. "Act in haste, repent at leisure" is an adage that is becoming ever more applicable to the results of our "activity," be it economic, political, or social.

Of course, life is neither mechanistic nor deterministic, and it often requires a lot of thought; working smart is what it is all about. Life can also be a capricious undertaking that requires us to get things just about right, rather than exactly right; "the best-laid schemes o' mice and men Gang aft agley" (from "To A Mouse," by Robert Burns). Therefore we have to be adaptive, responsive, and alert to what is actually happening.

Yet, many corporations still approach change programs, quality initiatives, world-class manufacturing efforts, and business process reengineering (BPR) as though we all occupied environments that can be unerringly structured and ordered. The fact is that Life and change can be and often are untidy items that need to be managed as best they can. Therefore, at this level, we offer *Relationship Dynamics* as an approach that will help managers to develop an understanding and thinking approach, rather than just "spinning their wheels," so that what needs to be managed can be managed.

We have sought to address a variety of concerns and, in so doing, have also touched on a multiplicity of issues that are not without an effect on our cohesiveness as a society and our competitiveness as an economy. We believe that is important for not only managers, but also social planners, politicians, and academics to appreciate that "private life" and "work" do not occupy separate limitation models. Both private life and work operate within the same global disciplines of power, sanction, change, and competition. Those of us, from whatever walk of life, who take cognizance of that, will be better able to understand the pressures for change that confront us and how best to respond.

Therefore, *Relationship Dynamics: Theory and Analysis* sets and develops a wide foundation in the preface and introduction. Within the Introduction we explain the current limitations of existing motivational models. We build on that understanding so that Relationship Dynamics' motivational model, represented by the Critical Life Diagram, is more easily seen as a more appropriate basis from which to construct an understanding of human association.

In the next chapter we touch on a range of issues. We

cannot ignore the widespread, growing uncertainty and disquiet over Western society's direction and development. A number of specific issues are identified; we go on to explain the competitive discipline of life (see the section on "the Life Cycle Dynamic" in Chapter 3). We clearly demonstrate that life is a relationship environment that requires certain qualities of our orientation towards association, qualities that are not promoted by current trends such as political correctness, "rightists," etc.

The following chapter, on Power and Change, is very important because it voices that power is both a requirement for sustainable existence and a product that arises out of relationship activity—a fact that, for some reason, has become politically correct to deny. In explaining both power and change we enhance our presentation concerning the competitive demands that life makes on us, all of the time—competition is something that will not go away, it is with us every second of our lives and in whatever guise of association we adopt. Thus, a successful response is nothing more, but nothing less, than an appropriate application of power.

In Chapter 5, "The Structure of Relationships," we begin our detailed explanation of relationship composition, points of orientation, and entity alignment, as well as concepts to do with relationship entity weight, flexibility, and direction. We also demonstrate both the high and detailed levels of problem analysis. Also, each relationship dimension and its component elements are explained. The concluding concept within this chapter is that of the "operational filter," which concerns the motivational predisposition that all relationship entities have.

The analysis part of the book begins with Chapter 6, entitled "Analyzing Relationships," and is completed in Chapter

7 on "Evaluating Relationships." At that point—before we draw matters to a close in Chapter 9, "Applying Relationship Dynamics,"—we look in Chapter 8 at how three world-class corporations have responded to change and the competitive demands of remaining viable. These three cases give us a good insight into how the nature of relationships between people and between organizations has a critical effect on the effectiveness of an organization's ability to identify, understand, and respond to the pressures for change in the environment that it occupies.

ACKNOWLEDGMENTS

I would like to thank Bob Wallace, our editor at The Free Press, for his immediate grasp and patient listening of "the message" that came to him from a voice deep in the Scottish Highlands. As fate would have it, it was a call made by me and answered, directly, by him.

I would also like to acknowledge Mike Anniss's belief in me, one that caused him to "take up sticks," so that our collaboration could be facilitated, even though it meant moving his family five hundred miles north into the land of the "Auld Enemy."

—James Musgrave

I would like to thank all of those at The Free Press who have assisted us, and James Musgrave for his support in the creation of *Relationship Dynamics* and for providing the conditions that enabled this book to be written.

—Mike Anniss

CHAPTER 1

INTRODUCTION

Relationship Dynamics springs from our deep conviction that relationships are the key to understanding the operation of the world in which we live. This belief springs from wide-ranging personal, commercial, and academic experience in many spheres including

- information technology
- psychology
- sociology
- manufacturing industry
- financial services
- health care
- strategic consulting
- education
- our own families and friends
- our own position in society

By *relationships* we do not mean simply an emotional perspective on the interaction between people. We mean a whole contributory matrix of factors that affect interactions

1

between people. These can be grouped under the headings of

- control
- emotion
- operation
- structure

Relationships are the lubricant that enables the social and economic environment to operate effectively. We believe that many different views of the social and economic environment are required to understand and manage it effectively. We do, however, contend that the other views cannot provide an effective understanding of the social and economic environment without first understanding the dimension of relationships.

In the psychological, sociological, and management literature, relationships have traditionally been seen on three main levels:

- As interpersonal interactions, where the style and nature of interactions has been evaluated, but not as the fundamental nature of relationships as building blocks for our social and economic development. These have been the focus of mainstream psychological and sociological investigation.
- As emotional constructs that have been treated in a populist fashion to attempt to understand situations involving such elements as love, hate, or sex.
- As a function of teams and working groups. These have been the main focus of management theory and practice investigation.

There are many different approaches and theories about these different aspects of relationships, but no single theory unites all of this information and provides a common base upon which to evaluate and understand any relationship.

Organization and management theory contains many references to relationship issues, but no systematic explanation through which those issues can be identified and evaluated. Interestingly, recent books and articles have begun to refer to the need to understand and manage relationships:

> Return on investment in relationships. We all invest in relationships. It's only human, off the job or on. But today's wisest firms, it seems, are those that are tops at consciously investing in relationships—steadily, over time, with a purpose and a passion. But even the stellar, pioneering outfits (Apple, MCI, Skonie, M2) don't try to measure it and that's a mistake.
>
> Tom Peters, *Liberation Management* (New York: Knopf, 1992)

> What is required is the adoption of measurement and research techniques which are available to transform many intangible aspects of service into tangibles.
>
> Richard Whiteley, *The Customer-Driven Company* (Reading, MA: Addison-Wesley, 1991)

> When our objectives change to include quality based objectives, they will place in front of all others the strategy of building solid and stable growth for the corporation through long-term relationships. In order to provide a safe and trusting atmosphere for that relationship to flourish, there are some ground rules, some changes from conventional thinking. For example, I expect both parties to make each other quite openly aware of their financial, material and intellectual dynamics. There will be a shared understanding and a mutual respect for the desire to embark down a planned and profitable path.
>
> John Fraser-Robinson, *Total Quality Marketing* (London: Kogen Page Limited, 1991)

These quotations reflect a belief that understanding and developing relationships is key to the effective operation of individuals and organizations. They are representative of many books on management trends published in the 1990s. This new emphasis on relationships, together with their dynamically task-driven formation and disbanding, has become a fundamental part of the ability of individuals and organizations to respond to the ever-changing demands of today's world. The ability to develop and manage relationships, within and between individuals and organizations, has become a key differentiator in today's competitive market place.

Although they identify relationships as a key dimension, the statements above do not provide any explanation of what relationships are, how they operate, or how they can best be managed.

In response, we have developed an approach called Relationship Dynamics that provides a powerful basis for understanding and managing relationships. The approach is a general one that applies to all relationships of whatever size and complexity.

Relationship Dynamics is relatively simple and intuitively accurate. Some people are suspicious of such simplicity. In practice, however, this simplicity and directness are what make the concept of Relationship Dynamics so powerful. It provides an understanding of a mechanism that we all deal with every day of our lives. The analytical steps of scoping, alignment, and profiling are ones that we all apply, to a greater or lesser degree, in managing our relationships every day. In *Relationship Dynamics* we have identified the key nature of relationships and presented it in a systematic format so that its clarity and power can be understood.

INTRODUCTION

We are not attempting to tell people how to behave in a particular way. We are, rather, providing people, groups, and organizations with an understanding and an analytical approach for managing all elements of their social and economic environment in a more effective manner. Relationship Dynamics will help you to understand and manage all the relationships you are involved in, ranging from personal relationships to complex ones between organizations and even nations.

Figure 1.1 was created as an opening gambit for a seminar weekend that we held in Verbier, Switzerland, during the Autumn of 1994. All of those present, including personnel from Hewlett-Packard, KPMG, A.B.B, and a Swiss computer consultancy called Xmit, reacted to this visual statement with both enthusiasm and studied interest. For Isidor, a

Figure 1.1
Making the dimensional shift

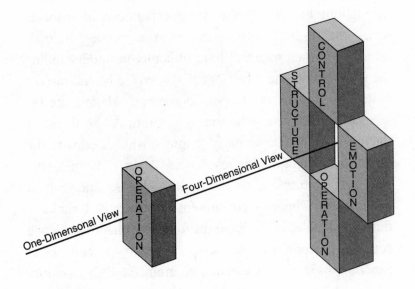

Swiss friend of mine who runs several resort hotels and acts as a consultant to a multifarious mix of hotel and leisure development groups, the figure "Making the dimensional shift" graphically portrayed and encapsulated his mind set. Isidor was very taken with Relationship Theory's presentation format as it assisted him to meaningfully represent and focus on the soft but critical elements that define a quality product.

Quality, for all industries, is developed and expressed largely as a function of the relationship that is established and developed between provider and customer. Returning to the diagram, this simple graphic illustrates the first adjustment that Isidor intuitively understood concerning the learning that his staff needed to achieve. During the short discourse that developed, Isidor explained how complex an exercise it was for his staff to qualitatively develop their skills and then translate them into real-time customer service improvements. Isidor said that the hardest task was enabling and assisting his staff to "see." He has found, throughout his twenty-plus years experience in management, that if staff cannot visualize the message in their mind's eye, then they will have difficulty in understanding the style and manner of change that needs to be embraced.

Relationship Theory's opening graphic, "Making the Dimensional Shift," sets the tone and captures the thrust of the message. The preliminary chapters, which deal with the Life Cycle Dynamic, Primary Tenets, Power, Change, Sanction, and Motivation, set the building blocks upon which Relationship Theory's constituent elements and explanations will be placed. Then, in the following chapters, we will consider the power-model perspective and the concept of Sanction, as they are elemental phenomena of the relationship mechanism. Relationship Theory (together with the defining parameters of its Primary Tenets, Change, Power, and Sanction) offers us both a macro and a micro framework for the understanding and management of both specific situations and generic strategies.

Current management theories are often not concerned with operational concepts such as the Life Cycle Dynamic, Change, Power, and Sanction. Much of the published work is anecdotally based. Causal analysis is often limited, and attempts to overcome that shortcoming are typified by huge investments in the production and processing of large volumes of detailed information. However, rather than capturing more meaning, those types of statistical exercise usually lead to a systems overload, where meaning is lost amid a sea of data.

Many management theories are limited because they overlook, do not consider, or fail to explain the following powerful realities:

- The base unit of human society is binary: two people entering into an operational association, i.e., forming a relationship.
- Our relationship forming ability represents mankind's main tactical and strategic adaptive response mechanism.
- In and for any society, power is a functional outcome that can only be created, managed, and applied as a consequence of a relationship process.

Instead, these management theories adopt a mechanistic approach focused on "hard data" points. That methodology assumes that it is possible to identify and measure all the physically distinct elements of customer and market interactions. However, that approach has excluded the study of the "soft" (and often more pertinent) interaction between organizations, customers, and markets.

As Figure 1.1 illustrates, Relationship Theory opens up our thought perspectives—the views that we adopt and the limits that we apply—to our operational environment. As Isidor plainly saw, quality is often a relationship "consequence" that contains what are considered to be the difficult "soft data" elements. We shall build a conceptual framework that will give those soft data points meaning and relevance and so enhance our understanding of the operational world that we contend with.

Expanding our view across four dimensions involves "thought innovation." That process causes a qualitative impact on one's view of the world. You will note from Figure 1.1 that the change demanded is an expansive one. It involves a reorientation that will develop and enhance the way we think. In other words, Relationship Theory will assist us to further develop our "thinking potential." As we have all experienced, developing our potential, be it physical, emotional, or mental, can and does have significant effects.

In addition, the difficult process of change management has been made even more arduous as a result of the way pressures for change now occur. The increased rate and volume of change has been accompanied by a transformation in the temperament, character, and methods through which change both formulates and is effected.

The multidimensional view includes a conceptual analysis of power that gives us an additional perspective. It offers all of us a unique insight into the increasing qualitative and quantitative effects that are putting ever greater pressure on the fabric of our social and operational structures. The multidimensional perspective enables us to more easily appreciate that society's "fabric" is composed of individuals in association and the various relationship networks that those associations represent and occupy. Those interwoven sets form and maintain our society.

It is prudent to bear in mind that the greatest danger to any society is one that can compromise society's ability to maintain its integrity. Consequently, it is crucial that whatever we do must be done in a way that enables us to hold together. In today's environment, we can better maintain that ability if we are able to rapidly assess, manage, and direct the forces of change. Therefore, how can we facilitate our grasp of this multidimensional view? The answer lies within and through *Relationship Dynamics: Theory and Analysis*.

CHANGES IN ANALYTICAL TECHNIQUES

When we wish to understand the basis of individual, social, and economic action, we must first understand how such phenomena can be identified, evaluated, and understood. Recent developments in the physical sciences have provided some fundamental changes in our understanding of how such phenomena come about and which tools and techniques can be used to analyze them. Organizations and individuals are also beginning to appreciate the need to develop a better understanding of the basis of human activity. However, we have found that existing methods of analysis do not capture the aspects that need to be understood.

In the physical sciences an appreciation of the nature of open systems has developed. These open systems cannot be adequately analyzed in terms of the traditional, deterministic, analytical models.

The natural sciences have rid themselves of the conception of objective reality that implied that novelty and diversity had to be denied in the name of immutable universal laws. They have rid themselves of a fascination with a rationality taken as closed and a knowledge seen as nearly achieved. They are now open to the unexpected, which they no longer define as the result of imperfect knowledge or insufficient control.

Ilya Prigogine and Isabelle Stengers, *Order Out of Chaos* (New York: HarperCollins, 1984)

The definition of open systems—systems that are fundamentally chaotic and nondeterministic in nature—has a major impact for their analysis. Closed systems, which operate at a basic level, are understandable in terms of standard classical analytical processes. Open systems, however, require analytic processes that can deal with their more chaotic and ultimately nondeterministic nature. *Relationship Dynamics* provides a new form of analysis complementary to the traditional, deterministic, reductionist approach that is at the heart of most current techniques for analyzing social and economic relationships. This open-system nature means that the relationships that we wish to understand are not purely deterministic, nor do they always react in the manner that we might expect them to. Before identifying how to approach this problem it is useful to look into some ideas that have developed in the very formal discipline of mathematical logic because they show that a general, heuristically driven approach is the basis of all real-world social analysis.

You mean the theory of games like chess. "No, no," he said. "Chess is not a game. Chess is a well defined form of computation. You may not be able to work out the answers, but in theory there must be a solution, a right procedure in any position. Now real games are not like that at all. Real life is not like that. Real life consists of bluffing, of little tactics of deception, of asking yourself what is the other person going to think I mean to do. And that is what games are about in my theory."

Jacob Bronowski relating a discussion with John von Neumann in The Ascent of Man (London: British Broadcasting Corporation, 1973), on the Theory of Games

This short discussion identifies a key element in the analysis of our social-world situations. The world in which we live and breathe, the social world, operates through a series of interactions that involve uncertainty and partial disclosure. Our ability to manage this world effectively depends on our ability to identify, understand, and then act on the basis of our perception of what is occurring in the situations that we encounter. That John von Neumann made this statement is particularly revealing. He is recognized as one of the founding fathers of the computer age, involved in the development of a tool that provides us with vast amounts of computational power whereby, given a determined starting point, we can "calculate" potential outcomes.

We have seen that human behavior is characterised by a high internal delay in preparation for deferred action. The biological groundwork for this inaction stretches through the long childhood and maturation of man. But deferment of action in man goes far beyond that. Our actions, as adults, as decision makers, as human beings, are mediated by value, which I interpret as general strategies in which we balance opposing impulses. It is not true that we run our lives by any computer scheme of problem solving. The problems of life are insoluble in this sense. Instead we shape our conduct by finding principles to guide it. We devise ethical strategies or systems of values, to ensure that what is attractive in the short term is weighed in the balance of the ultimate, long term satisfactions.

Jacob Bronowski in *The Ascent of Man* (London: British Broadcasting Corporation, 1973)

In understanding the nature of situations and responding to them we must understand the games and strategies that are being played, in order to interpret the information that we have. Relationship Dynamics provides a systematic format for laying bare the fundamental issues that are at play in any situation. By accepting this fundamental truth about the way in which we operate in a social environment, and then applying Relationship Dynamics, we generate the basic information needed to understand and manage any situation.

Relationship Dynamics does not try to provide a detailed explanation and analysis of all social and psychological phenomena; that would be an impossible task. Rather, it uses a relationship profile to analyze relationships in a manner that has practical utility. Such a relationship profile enables Relationship Dynamics to incorporate much of the knowledge that has been built up about social and psychological phenomena, in the form of relationship heuristics. These heuristics assist in understanding the manner in which relationships operate in the world because they help in identifying the course of action best suited to addressing any issues arising from a relationship.

CHAPTER 2

THE MOTIVATIONAL BASIS OF RELATIONSHIPS

We have said that current management theories, by focusing on the "hard elements" of organizations, such as processes and products, fail completely to contend with the "soft," less tangible aspects, such as perceived quality, emotional feelings, and concepts of power and responsibility.

Many theories compensate that limitation by investing in the production and processing of more and more detailed information, in an attempt to capture more meaning. That exercise leads to data overload and is no substitute for an appropriate analytical model. The reality is that our social and economic environment is nondeterministic, dynamic, and often chaotic. The inability of traditional theories to focus on the softer elements of interaction, with its "open systems" characteristics, means that they cannot capture the essence of motion and change adjustment that operates in all social and economic situations.

Business trends in the 1960s saw a focus on automation and new methods of measurement. In the 1970s attention was fixed on methods and systems. Customer Service, Added Value, and Total Quality Management exercises dominated the 1980s. The 1990s started with a focus on organizational structure and culture and on personal empowerment. Thus, each succeeding decade has had a characteristic style of management. The search for the talisman that will unlock the development of more successful and profitable organizations is continual.

Each of these characteristic approaches has resulted in schools of thought that are often contradictory and that compete for primacy. In addition, there is a general absence of rigorous and testable processes that, together with the lack of a defined structure, makes many of these theories nothing more than belief systems, i.e., products of emotional investments and statements of opinion. Consequently, business managers have had to choose between specific "views" of their situations, and usually adopt a "flavor-of-the-day" style of problem resolution. Logically, of course, the requirement is for a global approach that offers a holistic understanding within which to place these specific approaches. However, the basis for many of these approaches remains only anecdotal evidence and argument by analogy.

At the same time as anecdotally based proposals for organizational improvement have been popular, many organizations have been adopting quality programs based on statistical process control and detailed market analysis. Again, the belief seems to be that success lies in capturing profiles that are successful elsewhere, rather than developing an understanding of how and why they are successful. This often results in managers trying to apply situationally specific tools that do not fit every situation. For example, many of the approaches used in strategic market analysis, such as economic models and statistical process control, tend to provide data about the physical and financial operation of organizations. These methods, however, offer little insight concerning the softer elements of organizations such as culture, perceived quality, leadership, and openness. There has been no coherent model of individual, group, or organizational operation that can accept these different types of input and relate them to each other. This problem is clearly highlighted in the "quality" arena.

Statistical Process Control, a manufacturing-based approach based on the work of Shewart and Deming in the 1930s, is used to analyze the level of performance of products and processes. This provides a process-control view of situations, one which focuses on the production of a product as the key issue. The customer is acknowledged as a key element in this process, but the tools used are applicable to the analysis of products and processes rather than customers. Statistical Process Control makes it easy to measure the performance of a product or process, but difficult to measure the real impact of the product on the customer.

Another approach that attempts to capture and measure quality is Zero Defect. The danger of Zero Defect is that it creates a negative view of quality: if the product has *no* defects then it is *not* poor quality. Therefore, quality becomes, and is defined as, the absence of something rather than its presence. Zero Defect is a perfectly good goal for a production process, i.e., to build something with as low an error rate as possible. It defines a quality production process as an efficiency statement. We may achieve zero defects, but how do we keep a focus on what the product is supposed to deliver to the customer? The best engineered and produced product will not sell unless someone wishes to buy it. There is a continuing problem with the concept of Zero Defect quality because of this dichotomy. Peters (1992) defines product as: *product = product + intangibles*. It is the intangibles that often make a product successful.

SOURCES OF INDIVIDUAL MOTIVATION

Motivational theories attempt to generate a comprehensive theoretical framework for individual action. They also propose detailed heuristics for the interaction of these elements in the creation of internally generated purposeful action. Although this detailed analysis can provide a mass of information about the possible sources of individual action, the theories are usually overly complex and unable to unravel the contributions of each competing element. Further, they often suppose some form of rigorous operation by the individual in evaluating each of these elements prior to action. The vast field of motivational theory has proposed many different motivational mechanisms, some of which are summarized below.

Deep-Seated Drives of Sex, Aggression, and Ego (Freud, Adler)

These theories attempt to identify underlying emotional processes that interact with the normal daily operation of attempting to generate desired outcomes. These drives are deep seated and can lie hidden for many years before they emerge to impact on a person's behavior. Much of the "evidence" gathered for these theories is based on anecdote and speculative story telling. However, the concepts of arousal levels and primitive drives are often integrated into more modern approaches to motivation.

Need Theories (Maslow, Aldefer)

These theories attempt to identify the set of influences that drive behavior. Different sets have been identified by different theorists. Maslow introduced the concept of hierarchical organization of each motivational category with his famous pyramidal diagram of the hierarchy of human needs.

Hygiene and Motivational Factors (Herzberg)

Herzberg's theory distinguishes two levels of motivational influence: hygiene factors—elements associated with survival and the maintenance of a basic capability for living—and motivational factors—elements concerned with personal growth. This approach was aimed at the behavior of people in the work environment and was used to identify how people responded to differing changes in work conditions.

Self Actualization and Personal Growth (Rogers)

This approach focuses on the individual's ability to "grow" internally and through interaction with the environment, thus creating an identifiable sense of being in the world.

Social Learning Concepts (Rotter and Bandura)

This approach integrated the tactic of reinforcement of behavior patterns with the concepts of goal attainment and expectancy. It brought out that through interaction in the social environment we attempt to achieve specific goals and that behavior is reinforced or rebuffed through feedback generated in that social environment.

Expectancy and Achievement (McLelland and Atkinson)

These theories propose that there is a built-in predisposition for achievement. This predisposition could be identified and correlated with improved performance in school and the workplace. Atkinson extended the concept to include the converse, fear of failure.

Goal Setting (Locke and Latham)

This approach suggests that individuals must identify meaningful goals to which their action is directed. The impact of different types of goals and their interaction is investigated and related to specific types of behavioral outcomes.

Control Systems (Ford)

This approach takes many of the building blocks from previous theories and integrates them into an overall system to analyze motivation.

SOCIAL STRUCTURE

The fundamental unit of operation in society is the binary relationship. At the most fundamental level, it is represented by the association between a man and a woman. Also, it is through the formation of relationships that individuality will find expression and fulfillment. We will develop that point later in the text.

However, it is important to appreciate that it is through the operation of relationships that effective operation is achieved; the dogmatic assertion of individual independence has actually offered little utility as regards the development of appropriate response strategies. Therefore, within society we gain access to resources through interaction with others. All of the material resources we use are made available only through interaction with others. This dynamic drives society and creates an environment that enables us to initiate and manage our lives through a series of transactions with others. The need to interact with others links directly to the notion of dependence.

Within society, there is no such thing as total independence. The reality is that we all live in a state of managed interdependence. Indeed, it is this interdependence that we use to identify whether a society exists. People, groups, and organizations are all required to manage their interdependent relationships to a greater or lesser degree, depending on their capability and situation. Further, society provides a general level of facilities that adeptly conceal the underlying dependent situation of those who perform at the norm or better. This management is usually so effective that the nature of the interdependence that surrounds society's relationship structures is masked. One result is a focus on the end results of processes in society, rather than the full chain of dependent relationships that lead to those results. This demonstrates the lack of an intuitive understanding of the reality that we must manage the interdependent relationships in our lives rather than seek to become independent from them.

The more traditional Western focus on independence has made it difficult for many people to appreciate all of the elements that come to bear on their situations. Further, that lack of understanding leaves many people powerless to deal with their situation because they cannot understand the fundamental relationship issues and causes. The concept of an independent person, heavily promoted since the 1960s, has generated a limited view of situations based on the action of the individual rather than the larger set of issues based on all of the relationship dimensions. Relationship Dynamics recognizes that problem solving requires

- that each appropriate relationship be identified in order to understand any situation
- that all of the relevant dimensional elements be captured
- that the notion of interdependence be accepted, as this promotes a more appropriate view of situations, problems, and results
- that the notion of managed interdependence be accepted, in order to identify and understand the contribution of all parties in situations
- that relationships be seen as dynamic rather than static structures

This understanding of the structure of any action in society enables Relationship Dynamics to incorporate existing, more limited analytical approaches in an overall definition of how society works. From that base, Relationship Dynamics provides a more effective and complete mechanism for defining strategic developments and problem solving.

RELATIONSHIPS AND SUCCESSFUL OPERATION IN SOCIETY

There is powerful evidence that a basic strategy of cooperation is more successful than individualism. This evidence helps to explain why we humans have developed the group and social structures that have enabled us to adapt so effectively in the world.

The Benefits of Cooperation (Axelrod)

Robert Axelrod (1990) has developed an impressive body of research on the nature of cooperation. His research examines the nature and character of the relationships that develop when individuals interact. The basic question he asked was, "Are cooperative or selfish strategies more effective for success in a competitive environment?" He showed that where individuals interact, and there is a likelihood of that interaction persisting for future transactions, a cooperative strategy is the most effective.

Axelrod identified four optimum strategic elements for the development of productive relationships over time.

- Avoid unnecessary conflict by cooperating, as long as the other party does.
- Avoid provocation in the face of conflict.
- Practice forgiveness after provocation.
- Practice clarity of behavior so the other party can adapt to your behavior.

Key to the effectiveness of these strategies is the durability of the relationship between similar types of entities. Expectation of future operation of the relationship justifies cooperative operation at any point in time. Past operation of the relationship provides information on the strategies of both parties, information that enables effective choices at any future point in time. Axelrod's work identifies the need to see interactions between individuals within the context of an overall relationship that persists over time. Axelrod only investigated the strategic element of effective cooperative action. He did not go on to evaluate in greater detail the dynamic nature of relationships and transactions themselves. It is to this dynamic operation that Relationship Dynamics applies.

OTHER APPROACHES TO RELATIONSHIPS

There has been little attempt to provide an overall model of society based on all of the dimensions of relationships. Existing approaches have focused on narrower goals. There are many models based on sociological, psychological, information, and economic structures. These models provide information about some of the aspects of relationships, but all fail to provide a structure within which to place each contributing element and generate an overall view.

Symbolic Interactionalism (George Herbert Mead)

Symbolic Interactionalism is based on examination of the active interaction between individuals. It focuses on the exchange of symbols, pieces of meaningful information, that help to define the context and nature of a transaction between individuals. Symbolic Interactionalism acknowledges the importance of the relationships between individuals and/or groups, but does not explore the basic nature of those relationships. It focuses on the surface behavioral aspects of interaction, such as nonverbal communication, social rules, and forms of speech. These behaviors and forms of speech are often analyzed with reference to concepts such as power or formality with no specific definition of the underlying concepts.

Relationship Dynamics also takes the interaction between individuals as being a crucial component in the operation of individuals and groups in society. However, unlike Symbolic Interactionalism, Relationship Dynamics sees the underlying component dimensions of relationships as the key mechanism.

Modes of Social Interaction (Erving Goffman)

Goffman developed the concept of symbolic interaction further. His detailed analysis of the modes of social interaction led to his concepts of "focused interaction" and "unfocused interaction." Unfocused interaction occurs when people are interacting merely as a function of society, e.g., saying hello as you pass someone in the street. Focused interaction occurs when individuals directly attend to what the other is saying or doing. He showed how people differentiate between interactions with "markers" and distinguish between shared social behavior in "front regions" and private behavior in "back regions." Qualifier concepts of role and impression management were identified to show how people vary their behavior depending on how they wish to be seen by others.

Social Interaction here looks at the nature of the observable surface behaviors rather than the underlying structure of the relationship that may give rise to these behaviors. The difficulty with these concepts is that they are analyzed in terms of some underlying dimensions, such as power or approval, but these underlying dimensions are not themselves clearly defined.

Social Exchange (Peter Blau)

Blau introduces the concept of "coercive" verses "social" exchange. *Social exchange* refers to voluntary actions by individuals who are motivated by the returns they expected to receive. The concept of social exchange is thus developed in terms of the social benefits it brings: status, approval, group membership, etc. Social exchange is differentiated from economic exchange in that economic exchange usually has clearly specified outcomes whereas social exchange will often have unspecified outcomes. Social exchange requires trust because of this lack of specificity, but generates feelings, such as obligation and gratitude.

Blau contends that because economic exchange usually has a specified outcome and social exchange often has an unspecified outcome, they are fundamentally different dimensions. However, in identifying examples of the two dimensions, Blau shows how the reality is somewhat blurred. He gives the example of a banker making a loan without full collateral. He identifies this action as having elements of both economic and social exchange, since the outcome is specified, but also dependent on a promise of future unknown performance.

In Relationship Dynamics these two dimensions are not seen as intrinsically different; they are examples of exchange and interaction. However, they operate with reference to all the component dimensions of relationships and represent discrete positions on a continuum of interaction types. The predisposition to labeling specific types of relationship *social* or *economic* forces a perspective that may not be correct. In Relationship Dynamics the relationship is defined in terms of its particular goals, be they social, economic, or a combination of both. The relationship dimensions of

- emotion
- operation
- control
- structure

provide a framework that enables any relationship to be analyzed in a fashion that captures its social or economic characteristics, as well as many additional elements.

Transactional Analysis (Eric Berne)

Berne contends that relationships and social interaction are necessary for normal human operation. This need is addressed by the development of a series of *transactions* between individuals that provide *strokes* for each other; that is, they provide positive recognition of the other's presence. These two concepts, *social interaction* and *stroking to develop one's self-image* are at the core of the Transactional Analysis process. Berne also identifies three ego states that correspond to particular ego states within an individual:

- *Parent:* states that resemble those of parental figures
- *Adult:* states that are autonomously directed toward objective appraisal of reality
- *Child:* states similar to those developed in childhood

Berne contends that at any point in time an individual in a social transaction will take on one of these three ego states. These three ego states are then used as the basis for problem identification in relationships. Individual behaviors within transactions are analyzed for their type: Parent, Adult, or Child. Where problems occur in these transactions the identification of inappropriate use of an ego state is used to show what the problem is and how it can be resolved.

Transactional Analysis, like Relationship Dynamics, sees social transactions as necessary for effective operation in society. Transactional Analysis is, however, limited in its scope. It uses the Parent/Adult/Child concept to identify dysfunctional outcomes and their consequences, but these apply mainly to problems in relationships between individuals. It provides nothing to explain the relationship problems when there is no problem with ego states in relationships. Relationship Dynamics provides a much more complete description of relationships and includes the elements covered by Transactional Analysis within the emotion and control dimensions.

REDEFINING THE PROBLEM

First, it is possible to identify distinct elements for analysis such as customers, markets, and organizations; and rigorous measures can be taken of these elements and their interactions. From that base a series of analytical techniques have been developed that focus on the mechanistic interactions between those elements. Most of these techniques have been developed from a manufacturing base of defined processes, ones that employ a deterministic cause-and-effect profile.

Second, there is a much richer set of interactions between organizations, customers, and markets. These interactions can be understood in terms of satisfaction, perceived quality, and emotional responses. Many approaches identify this key dimension, but do not provide an underlying theory or structure to identify and define these softer elements.

A new approach is required to bring these two different approaches together in a common theory. This new perspective must identify all of the elements of operation that apply to individuals, groups, and organizations including the intangible aspects. It must accommodate the successful approaches that currently exist and place them in a more appropriate context. It must provide a basic structure that is flexible and can dynamically respond to the ever-changing nature of organizations, customers, and markets.

THE SOLUTION: A FOCUS ON RELATIONSHIP DYNAMICS

We act in the world within a series of operational environments in order to achieve the goals we wish to reach. These operational environments have characteristics of their own, but they exist, essentially, to generate the desired outcomes for the individuals involved. The generation of these operational environments requires both the formation of relationships and feedback from those relationships.

The anecdotally based, intuitive approaches to quality, satisfaction, and excellence capture internal feelings about situations. The more formal statistical process-control approaches capture information about the operational environments we have generated. They both, therefore, capture meaningful information but fail to provide a coherent model with which to integrate that information into a meaningful whole.

Relationship Dynamics provides the framework to identify and integrate these different elements. It therefore provides a base from which organizations, customers, and markets can be analyzed.

THE DEVELOPMENT OF A NEW
MOTIVATIONAL MODEL

This vast range of proposed mechanisms demonstrates that there is no single, simple definition of the motivational forces that drive individuals. There is, however, general agreement in most of these theories that there are at least two key aspects of motivation: the external impact of material needs and the internal impact of emotional needs. Taking those two elements as a base, Relationship Dynamics has been able to build an operationally relevant model of the actions of individuals in relationships.

The motivational structure of Relationship Dynamics shows how relationship formation and operation are necessary, in the real world, for the satisfaction of both our external and internal motivational elements. Humans are social animals who satisfy all their needs through relationships with others. In analyzing the nature of relationships, it becomes clear that they form a key element in the satisfaction of the internal emotive needs of individuals. These basic needs, which we have called the critical drives, can be described as:

• self-esteem and dignity—to be valued
• a sense of belonging—to be cared for and part of a group
• a sense of identity and capability—to produce an individual contribution

Relationship Dynamics builds upon that basic motivational definition by making it clear

• that the individual's emotional dimension, the Critical Drive State, is fundamental to all action.
• that this internal dimension, as well as external material needs, is addressed through the formation and operation of relationships.
• that the goals of individuals must be seen in the context of the relationships they form in order to satisfy these internal and external dimensions.

Relationship Dynamics identifies the primacy of relationships in generating purposeful action to meet both internal and external goals. Thus, the formation of individual goals is intertwined with the development of shared goals in relationships. This sharing element in goal formulation and achievement is key because there will be few if any situations where individuals do not have to work with other entities to achieve their goals. The motivational model that is derived from this process, and that is based on shared outcomes, enables individuals or groups to focus on the activities they must undertake to operate effectively. Further, it provides an external and objective basis from which the effect of internal motivation can be understood.

A deeper analysis of an individual's motivation relies on each individual's perception of his or her internal state and the ability to align this understanding with an external model or view of that state. The difficulty here is that there is no way of knowing how well aligned these internal and external views are. This has resulted in the development of the many motivational theories identified above, and many associated therapeutic regimens that are often in fundamental conflict with each other.

Relationship Dynamics is based on the assumption that the lack of a complete and coherent theory of interaction is inevitable because the individualized internal dimension defies deconstruction, and therefore yields little detailed understanding of individual motivation. With that limitation in mind, Relationship Dynamics states that the most effective way to manage motivational forces is to focus on the operational issues of life and the relationships that must be entered into to achieve operational goals. By focusing on operational goals, a shared understanding of operation can be developed and used as the basis for the effective analysis of situations. This explicitly defined base provides a much more useful starting point for the effective operation of individuals and groups within the inevitably interactive social environment.

THE CRITICAL DRIVE STATE

The Critical Drive State model provides a motivational framework that gives us an external and objective basis from

Figure 2.1
The Critical Life Diagram

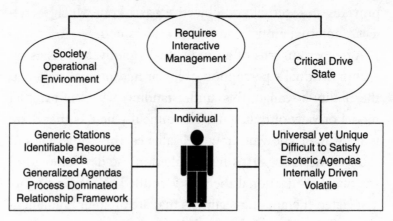

which the effects of internal motivation can be understood—the dynamic of managed interdependence.

The Critical Life Diagram, Figure 2.1, depicts the underlying constraints, drives, and tensions that govern the need for
the relationship framework and human association.

- It portrays the intrinsic interdependence and the interactive
  relationship that exists concerning the satisfaction of our
  Critical Drive State and the operational world we live in.
- An understanding of those interactive constraints, drives,
  and tensions is crucial for the formulation of appropriate
  management strategies that we can then apply to the relationships we form to achieve our goals.

Thus, the Critical Life Diagram, Fig 2.1, shows that Relationship Dynamics theory concerning the understanding
of motivation starts with the analysis of how individuals
come into and form their associations. That means we look
at individuals in society, in terms of the relationships they

form, rather than at the subordinate structures such as organizations or groups. That analysis is made with an acknowledgment that all association is underpinned by the need to satisfy the Critical Drive State. Therefore, we propose that meaningful understanding of individual motivation and interaction must involve the identification of the underlying relationship dimensions upon which that cooperative and multidimensional action is based.

Let us consider the right-hand side of the Critical Life Diagram more closely as regards the complex nature of our internalized sense of self.

- The Critical Drive State is universal (it is our sense of self).
- Critical Drives may override the physical survival drives.
- Individuals need to satisfy their Critical Drive State in order to experience a sense of well being.
- The Critical Drive State agendas are veiled, specific, and difficult to satisfy.

Figure 2.2
The right-hand side of the Critical Life Diagram

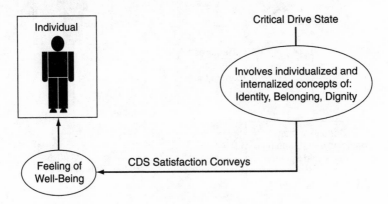

We all have an internalized sense of self. However, what that actually is and contains is highly subjective and hidden from view; what makes you, you is complicated, internalized, and can probably never be fully understood. Therefore, it is important to remember that our sense of self, illustrated as the Critical Drive State, can only remain satisfied and in balance through, and as a result of, the relationships that we form and the outcomes that those relationships generate.

In looking at the left-hand side of the Critical Life Diagram we can more fully appreciate the need to form relationships.

- Our social existence and the need to satisfy our Critical Drive State provides the initial orientation for forming relationships.
- Society is our operational environment in which we seek relationships, because through that process individuals satisfy their Critical Drive State.

Figure 2.3
The left-hand side of the Critical Life Diagram

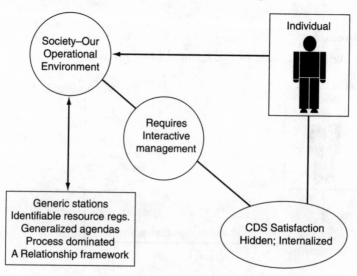

- Failure to satisfy the Critical Drive State will, at some point, compromise relationship integrity.
- We are all challenged by the need to manage the interaction that arises between the need to satisfy our Critical Drive State and the specific demands of the relationships we actually form.

Thus, Relationship Theory's motivational model provides the initial orientation concerning the framework that we have built to better understand how we form the relationships we do and to what effect. The most simple but powerful understanding of all is the understanding that every successful and happy "me" is dependent upon the establishment of an operationally sound, effective, and successful "us." We will gain further insights into the power of this orientation for analysis by looking at the underlying constraints that affect change management programs and our Critical Drives.

CRITICAL DRIVES AND CHANGE MANAGEMENT

The challenges that confront change management exercises are complex and often fraught with difficulties. However, many of those difficulties will arise, and will be articulated in and through, the relationship interaction between the people implementing the change and those charged with adopting and working with that change. Much of the qualitative information about the change will reside in what we call "soft data."

Figure 2.4, below, illustrates that a successful change management strategy will be one that manages both the alteration of the operational environment and the attendant

Figure 2.4
Change management

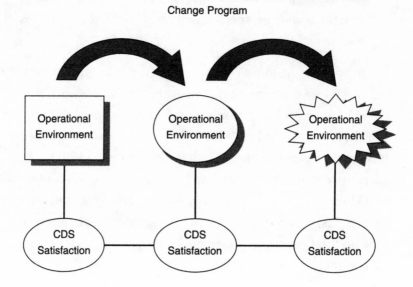

Change Management — Management of Relationships

Change Program

Operational Environment

Operational Environment

Operational Environment

CDS Satisfaction

CDS Satisfaction

CDS Satisfaction

adjustment in the relationship model. The latter is crucial because only in that way will the critical human entities retain Critical Drive State satisfaction.

- Change management will always involve operational and Critical Drive issues.
- A successful change management program will understand and accommodate the relationship models within which the change process will be initiated, transformed, and consolidated, so that Critical Drive State satisfaction is attained.

Critical Drive State satisfaction is fundamental. Though the Critical Drive State can withstand temporary dissatisfaction (we can all do things we do not want to do or like doing, up to a point), a change will be successful only if it ensures that the Critical Drive State of those who must make the change work is satisfied. A failure to make that management adjustment will jeopardize the viability and integrity of the new relationship model on which all the changed processes, products, and underlying improvements in profitability depend.

It is important that the key relationship sets, such as employees, customers, and shareholders do not become alienated, as that would have a major influence on the eventual outcome of the change program.

Therefore, it is neither operationally relevant nor useful to try to evaluate the internalized motivational drives that make individuals "tick." What does give operational utility and is intrinsically important, as regards individual satisfaction and change management success, is gaining an understanding of how the relationship model has been formed and operates.

Relationship Theory gives us that perspective. It enables us to identify the basis upon which a relationship model has been formed. Therefore, it will facilitate our appreciation of those areas that will embrace the change well and those that will not. That utility is gained because central to the Critical Drive State motivational model are the relationship dimensions upon which association has been constructed and operated so that Critical Drive State satisfaction is achieved.

Figure 2.5, "Change: The management of revelation," illustrates the multidimensional interaction that underpins human association and how those variables can appear to be "new" as a result of a change in one's operational environment. This illustration also provides us with a format to take our consideration of the concept of managed interdependence further.

- Figure 2.5 is an illustration of the powerful management issues that often arise as a result of an individual confronting a Life Change.
- Figure 2.5 shows that a Life Change's greatest impact can actually result from a reorientation of perception.
- This exemplifies that the interdependency of life is always open to the process of "revelation" because of the nature of the change—in this case from work to long-term care.
- Therefore, the crucial management of Critical Drive State satisfaction remains, but perhaps has been made a much more complex and difficult task.

Fig. 2.5 shows a dramatic juxtaposition: the individual at work versus the individual in care. The classic perception is that an individual in long-term care is in a dependent situation, as opposed to the independent individual in gainful employment. The reality is that both are in interdependent positions with neither being more or less "independent" than the other. However, in analyzing the perceived move, as shown above, some fundamental issues are revealed as having to do with change and Critical Drive State. Let us consider some of those points.

- The person in work probably chose his work relationship; the person in long-term care probably was forced to accept that he needed care.
- The concept of work intrinsically has a notion of fair exchange, i.e., work is a noncharitable process.
- Being cared for has little to do with fair exchange; rather it is often seen as a "charitable" process of "doing good."

THE MOTIVATIONAL BASIS OF RELATIONSHIPS

Figure 2.5
Change: the management of revelation

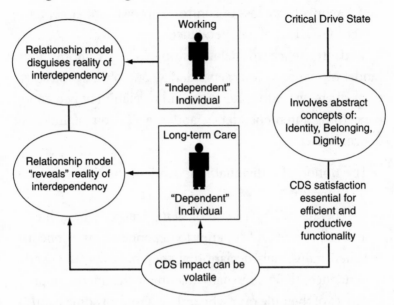

- The "worker" probably has a reasonable amount of knowledge and some control over his operational position within the working relationship.
- The "patient" is often subject to "professional expertise," in which the caregivers are deemed to have the greater competency to exercise control over the relationship. The patient is, fundamentally, disempowered within traditional care models.

It is obvious that the move from work to long-term care is likely to involve, for a time, the unbalancing of the individual's Critical Drive State, and therefore likely to expose the person to the risk of engaging a range of negative feelings. However, each of the relationships depicted is in an interdependent situation. What is different is the basis of association. That difference reflects the respective constituent components upon which each relationship is based. The move into care involves a loss of control, approval, and acceptance rather than a loss of independence.

With reference to Relationship Theory's motivational model of managed interdependency, one of the central features of change is the alteration and revelation of perception concerning interdependency and the illusion of independence. In fact

- The notion of individual independence is a very modern day concept.
- Independence, as a state of being that can be achieved and is different and superior to dependence, is erroneous.
- When individuals declare that they have lost their independence, they are usually making a statement about an aspect of their life over which they have lost some control; they are referring to a diminished ability to manage and exercise control over certain aspects of their life.
- When we are able to exercise an acceptable degree of control over the myriad of relationships that make up our life, we often experience a sense of satisfaction and prowess. This should not be confused with independence.
- "Independence" of any sort is always a trade-off. To be independent of poverty, we will be *dependent* on those relationships that enable us to maintain a good income.
- Societal living facilitates the crucial and fundamental process of relationship formation. Living in close association maximizes an individual's opportunity to establish a successful relationship set, one that is, broadly, operationally effective and satisfying.
- It is important to note that the basis upon which a rela-

tionship is formed will predispose the relationship interaction that follows.

Thus, the operational character as well as the perceived or
"revealed" nature of any change program will have to be
managed; this is often the most difficult aspect of the exercise. The consequences of both parts of the dynamic, operations and perceptions, will have real-time impacts. One way
or another, successful change management will have to

• take account and be appreciative of an organization's relationship model even though that is usually a composite
  conglomeration of relationship sets, each with a variation
  concerning its basis for internal and external interaction.

CHAPTER 3

RELATIONSHIP THEORY

THE LIFE CYCLE DYNAMIC

The Life Cycle Dynamic is a basic concept of the operational explanation of human association. The Life Cycle Dynamic defines animate life as involving *a process that attempts to meet the needs of revitalization and propagation.*

That is a very simple but powerful statement describing the dynamic process of life. It does not indicate good or bad, nor does it define better or worse. Nor does this definition suggest that there is a determinate outcome. Indeed, implicit in that statement are ideas concerning the maintenance of vitality, viability, competition, and continuation— the very goals of every commercial enterprise and management team.

Those concepts are also instrumental to the development of operational definitions concerning Change, Power, and Sanction. Let's see how all this knits with the demands and forces that affect the development of effective management strategies. It is undeniable that Life must be in a viable and sustainable form in order to exist and thrive. If a current form of association or organizational structure's viability is compromised, it is in danger of ceasing to exist. Therefore, what is necessary to maintain that viability? That answer involves a complex interplay of elements that are best depicted by the concept of *revitalization,* defined as *"the process through which one is enabled to sustain a viable form of existence."*

Revitalization is undertaken and appears in many forms: the birth of children, the reorganization of a company, the hiring of a new baseball coach. In whatever guise, the process is about maintaining a viable form of existence. Also, within this framework, one appreciates that degradation must always be combated, given that animate beings and the associations they form are subject to a range of change pressures and will need to be able to update themselves. Therefore, it is also clear that revitalization will cause demand pressures to build that must be reacted to. Let's examine how those stresses develop.

Essentially, revitalization is an animate process of dynamic renewal, to make new again. Also, for us it is never an exact duplicating process. Rather, it is one that generates varied similarity. Genetic differences, varied environments, altered niches, technological development, all those compound the variation effect. The central question is, how does one respond?

Insects respond to the pressures, demands, and consequences of the Life Cycle Dynamic with a huge birth rate, short intergeneration time lapse, and mutation. We don't; we can't. Our generation time lag, variation, and mutation are far too slow to be an effective adaptive response mechanism. Therefore, how do we respond? The answer is obvious; humans respond to the pressures, demands, and consequences of the Life Cycle Dynamic through and by the relationship mechanism. That ability allows three significant functions.

- It enables the variation of individual resources and talent to be pooled and applied.
- It provides an opportunity to create mass and generate outcomes that are greater than the sum of the individual entities.
- Through it power applications can be created, developed, managed, and applied.

Relationship Theory states: *"We can only understand our operational environment through an appreciation of the relationship dynamic."* That statement leads us to Relationship Theory's four Primary Tenets.

- Our social and economic environments are best managed as a result of an analysis and understanding of how relationships are formed and operated.
- The relationship mechanism reveals that our "living" process requires us to acknowledge, accept, and embrace the intrinsic interdependency of our association.
- Our adaptive capability to respond to the Life Cycle Dynamic is represented by and effected through the relationship mechanism. It is through our ability to form, manage, and sustain successful relationships that we are able to make and apply competitive responses to the challenges that life throws at us.
- The social, economic, and physical pressures caused by the Life Cycle Dynamic result from the continued need for regenerative action and consequent reaction. In other words, engagement of the Life Cycle Dynamic's competi-

tive challenge is responsible for the "change pressures" that affect our physical, social, and economic systems.

In the last of those tenets is contained the definition of *change*. We will explore that conceptual statement at more length later. For now, it is important to note that Relationship Theory's primary tenets demonstrate a fundamental acceptance that change is an integral *consequence* of the life process. The more society has developed its prowess to provide for its populations' *baseline needs,* the greater the operational challenge has become centered on the management of the *"soft" elements.*

We operate in an environment dominated by open systems and continual change. In industry and commerce the ability to operate efficiently and produce "perfect" products at low prices has led to a new focus on the "softer" elements of the social and economic environment. These changes require us to develop a more effective understanding of the manner in which we develop and sustain relationships and to focus much of our attention on optimizing the relationships that we have.

In addition, the traditional approaches to understanding the operation of relationships have tended to focus on narrow areas of implementation, rather than providing an overall understanding of the operation of relationships. As a result, relationships are traditionally analyzed in a partial manner dependent upon the nature of the relationship issue being analyzed. Motivation has usually been evaluated in terms of the internal forces at play within an individual. The reality of the human being as a social animal is that the external interactions required to satisfy internal drives are key to the generation of purposeful action. The challenge is to develop an effective understanding of the whole environment within which we operate as individuals, groups, organizations, or nations. Relationship Dynamics provides that understanding and an analytical process for applying that understanding in the real world.

The challenge posed by the "soft" elements has laid bare the need to expand our focus of analysis beyond the process methodology. Relationship Theory offers all of us an opportunity to develop a more effective comprehension of the methods employed to form and sustain successful relationships. Also, that appreciation will go a long way toward enabling us to evaluate our existing relationships and optimize their operation and effectiveness.

Moving on to the second primary tenet, *interdependency* is intrinsic to the Life process. That means, simply, that no one is an island. Every meaningful act, need, or endeavor requires an interactive relationship with some other entity. Indeed, it is almost impossible to imagine even the most "individualized" agenda being effected without forming a relationship with some other party. Relationship Theory acknowledges, accepts, and embraces the intrinsic interdependency of Life, and therefore uses the relationship as its starting point for analysis. The individual and individuality are not denied, they are merely redefined as "unique" resources that we bring to the relationships that we form.

For example, one might have the potential to become the greatest football player who has ever played, but that individual's potential can only have a chance of being realized if an appropriate relationship set is formed that will enable that potential to become manifest. Logically, "One can't play football without a team."

As the third primary tenet outlines, humanity's adaptive

capability is dependent upon the effective operation of relationships. Empirically, that is indisputable. Of course, that fact also enforces the reality that Life is an interdependent process. Our obligations and responsibilities can only be met through an understanding that there must exist, and be preserved, an underlying capability and willingness to enable those obligations and responsibilities to be met.

Consider. Many of us in the West appear to enjoy a personal freedom greater than that available within other societies. However, that freedom is not available because it is an "inalienable right." That freedom is there because there are a myriad of relationships that have been formed, developed, and managed so that our society has the socioeconomic prowess to provide its members with that freedom and strength. Our freedom of access and movement; our ability to consume and purchase; our capability to provide for the needy; our ability to protect ourselves and our way of life; all that is a capacity and provision that is dependent not on the right to those things but on relationships within our society—those that

- acknowledge and accept those obligations and responsibilities concerning personal freedoms.
- have and maintain both a willingness and an ability to ensure that those "rights" can be defined, identified, provided, and delivered.

In other words, everything we have results from relationships that have been formed to enable that provision to be made. The freedoms and "rights" we enjoy do not exist as a right, nor does the status of "right" by itself enable us to have them. A provision, of whatever form and type, can only be made if there exists a relationship model that has the ability to make and deliver it.

It is important for us to realize that the West was not made strong by making the individual "prime." Rather, its strength has rested on its ability, as a society, to form a more successful and sustainable relationship framework. It is important to appreciate that the West's skills and power were dependent on the direction of development of its relationship framework.

That framework moved, throughout its period of accelerating ascendancy, toward a more flexible and dynamic basis of association—a form of association that was able to benefit from the internal disciplines that existed within individuals, and which they brought to relationship formation. That disciplined quality meant that

- the commonality of the conventions, upon which those internal disciplines were based, greatly reduced the costs of policing, motivating, and organizing the basis of association in the West's populations.
- the West's more flexible relationship model was able to rapidly realign the operational and economic goals that underpinned and drove that basis of association.

The above account principally for the West's ability to realize the interdependent needs of its populations more effectively. By way of a brief empirical example of comparison, the Soviet Union and much of Eastern Europe had a very prescriptive and highly inflexible model of association. Its Socialist/Communist political ideology effectively set a "blueprint" for socioeconomic association that demanded a form of policing focused on the "political correctness" of that association rather than on the operational effectiveness of the outcomes that were required. That quality contributed largely to the socioeconomic implosion that resulted.

Figure 3.1
Life: a relationship environment

Societal living maximizes the opportunity for relationship forming. The opportunity for human association to yield successful applications is facilitated by that social framework. Thus, society's operational environment requires the spread of human resources to generate, as an aggregated function of society's relationships, responses that fundamentally meet the needs of society.

The individuals who form and operate within those relationships represent the wealth of resource talent that a society's relationship mechanism can draw upon.

Globally, the ability to form relationships, coupled with a population's diversity and range of individual talent, has facilitated mankind's ability to develop appropriate and sustainable responses to changing conditions over time. A successful society is one that is able to draw on its diverse talents so as to generate responses that overcome or meet the challenges thrown against it. We should note two points, one of which is a statement about consequence.

- Diversity is not a performance statement in itself; it simply means that different talents, levels of talent, etc., exist and can be drawn upon.
- One result of success is a decrease in diversity.

Therefore, it is critical that a society retain and invest in viable and responsive relationship models. Relationship Theory promotes just that as it offers an understanding of both the relationship dimensions and the applicability of the various component and resource requirements that apply.

Every society is faced with the difficulty of striking a balance between the need for structure and fixity and the degree to which it accommodates change. Too much investment in structure and control can disable a society, because it can become overprescriptive and inflexible. Such a process will cause a society to begin to lose its integrity and responsive capability. If that continues, the society will become dysfunctional and lose its viability. When that occurs, a society decays, may reform, or dies out. That last point should alert us to the need to recall the lessons that should have been learned by the fall of the Soviet Union.

Russia has paid and is still paying for the consequences of a totalitarian experience that was set by its Marxist political cliques. A question that comes to mind, as a result of Russia's totalitarian and collectivist experience, is, "Will political correctness, with its wealth of prescriptive demands and agendas, its focus on rights and its disregard of the underlying relationship requirements for a successful society, not pose a similar threat to the United States and the West?"

Theoretically, a society's or organization's prevailing relationship model will contain a range, from the best to the worst, of the relationship combinations currently devised. An analysis of that model will enable one to understand the specificity of its relationship dimensions. The nature of that specificity will provide very detailed data concerning both the extent and the limits of the response that a society's or organization's current relationship model can generate. This is particularly valuable to the process of planning Change agendas.

For example, it may be that the change factors being proposed will be beyond an organization's ability to respond—all relationship models have bounds. Therefore an analysis based on Relationship Theory can provide an invaluable insight and an opportunity to reevaluate both the content of the change program and the current specificity of one's relationship model. Perhaps the change agenda can and should be altered; perhaps the relationship model will be realigned; perhaps both.

Relationship Theory states that there is an indisputable reality concerning the operation of life and any form of organization: we may have the right product, we might have the correct process, and we probably have the relevant people, but do we have the appropriate relationship model through which the product, process, and people operate? A useful insight on that question can be gained by looking at Relationship Theory and applying its analytical process.

INDIVIDUALITY

It is usually at about this point in the proceedings that we begin to hear the cry about individuality and concern expressed: "Where does the 'Me' aspect come in?" After all, the argument starts, isn't Life about doing what one wants to do, when one wants to do it, and according to one's preference? To that simplistic view and argument, the answer is obviously "No." How can it be?

The act of Life and living is an interdependent process. We have to engage in mutual strategies to some degree in order to live. Life is a process of mutual exchange—even anarchists form "societies" to advance their beliefs because as individuals they can go nowhere. Yes, the search and opportunity for individuals to realize their potential and achieve their goals has played a powerful role, but that role has been primarily catalytic.

The West broadly limits central planning by maximizing the self-regulatory and autonomous view of individuals as regards their needs and the structural limitations on how they can and will satisfy their wants. In other words, Western culture has utilized the "homeostasis effect" concerning the self-regulatory actions that come into play as a result of the intrinsic limitations that an individual or population will have or will impose upon itself. That is in direct contrast to the heavy investment that Socialist and totalitarian societies have to make to ensure compliance with their "politically correct" creeds and profiles of "allowable" behavior.

That means that a type of "guidance" has underpinned the Western concepts of *individuality*, the *pursuit of individual goals*, the *attainment of personal freedom*, and the *development of individual potential*. That "understood" guidance has enabled the West to safely (most times) engage those concepts as dynamos that have imparted and still impart terrific amounts of energy to and motivation for its societies' interactive relationship models.

"Individualism" has been both a fuel and an essential ingredient in the creation of an operational model that has enabled the West to attain and maintain a vital and dominant society for the last four centuries. Historically, that less prescriptive focus has enabled a vital and robust culture to develop, one that has been able to handle change well and respond to the increasing disposition of the pressures for change that have confronted it—especially the vast quantitative and qualitative change in the character of the demands arising out of population pressure, increased social mobility, technological development, and war.

Therefore, at this point in the West's history, it is worthwhile for us to note and consider the potential impact of a very vociferous, self-righteous, but "media powerful" element within our own society. This group, "the politically correct," fill the airwaves with their views on issues such as affirmative action, diversity, historical balance, collective guilt, and compensation.

Indeed, their intense focus on "rights" and legislation as the mechanism whereby social interaction and development will take place represents, in many ways, the "new totalitarianism." The PC agenda of icons has largely been formed out of populist opinions, and their advocates seek compliance to their demands through a program of emotional blackmail, underpinned by an array of actual and implied sanctions. It seems somewhat ironic that our own form of "social prescribers" may yet represent more of a challenge to Western societal prowess than that offered formerly by Eastern

European Socialism, Communism, and, of late, by the growing economies of the Pacific Rim countries.

Relationship Theory does not focus on the "should" but on the "is." Relationship Theory enables us to better understand that "interwoven network" of individuals that together form our social constructs. In order to understand and learn we need to know how those constructs come together, how they operate and how they change. That understanding will also give us a definition of our underlying operational structures and the way in which those structures operate and interact.

ASPECTS OF CHANGE

Relationship theory's fourth primary tenet contains an intrinsic appreciation of what change is and how it comes about. Change is defined as *that qualitative and/or quantitative effect that results from the Life Cycle Dynamic's need to initiate regenerative action and consequential reaction.*

It is important to note the term "need." Of course change can result in a less vital or even a more degenerated formation. Therefore the point here, about human society as well as any form of organic group, is that successful and continued existence results from a process over time that has resulted in more successful than unsuccessful change responses.

Therefore, this definition interprets change as being the result of the process of renewal and the effort to maintain viability. In other words, change does not arise of itself nor should it be sought as an end in itself. Rather, organic and social change occurs as a function of the need for revitalization.

That qualitative statement enables us to see a simple reality, one that appears to warrant scant consideration in both main-stream management and socioeconomic theories. Tradition-ally, there is an acceptance that "Yes, we are always changing," but there appears to be little appreciation of why and how. Those are questions that need answering, and Relationship Theory provides the most appropriate "way in" at both the macro and micro levels of socioeconomic experience.

Once this definition of change has been stated it seems ob-vious. Yet, the fundamental importance of it seems to be rapidly lost amongst the various implementation strategies and theories surrounding reengineering, motivation, quality, and hard-data formulation. However, what could be more rel-evant than knowing how and why something has come about. Surely it is important to appreciate what, where, why, and how a relevant response should be made and composed?

As stated in the definition, one aspect of change is "re-generative action." That should be fairly and intuitively ap-parent. Life needs to recreate itself, in some form, in order to perpetuate and prosper. Viable life is characterized by a vital, effective, and responsive regenerative capability. That is the same characteristic that depicts any successful company. Therefore, this definition is as applicable to industry as it is to any other socioeconomic endeavor.

The other aspect of change is *consequent reaction*. This is important because there most of the operational challenge to change arises. Consider man and woman. They "regener-ate" by conceiving and bearing a child—they reproduce, a straightforward process that they can undertake, initially, with little dislocation to their lifestyle, level of expertise, and resource requirements. However, once the reproduction process has "borne fruit," we find that an immediate and rapid reaction is required. Bearing in mind that the baby is not a clone, or an exact image, or a duplicate, what has the regenerative action created? It has

- introduced a similar but different individual into the environment and so has diversified the constituent human resources upon which the relationship mechanism will be able to draw.
- caused an increase in resource demand—there is now one extra body to feed, clothe, entertain, educate, and prepare for the world.
- altered the flexibility of the socioeconomic strategies that the parents can employ to meet their respective and joint needs.
- demanded that the parents consider and undertake new roles and obligations, e.g., the process of bonding, setting an example, teaching life skills, acting as friend, protector, nurturer, and disciplinarian.
- made the "life unit" more vulnerable but also more vital—the former is an immediate concern, the latter a longer-term benefit.
- changed both the number and type of relationships that now operate.

Thus, the major effort associated with Change lies in the *consequent reaction* that has to be undertaken in order to successfully manage the regenerative action.

In a commercial setting, an appropriate and successful Change is more likely to occur if there is an awareness of the need to revitalize and an ability to do so. When there is such a need it is usually obvious from indicators such as negative profits or dissatisfied customers. However, the challenge that Change often brings is not what needs to be done, i.e.,

Change here and there, but in implementing that Change (a vital part of the reaction program)—the "how" part is always more tricky.

As we have seen, successful regenerative action will increase our vitality at the same time that it usually exposes us to an immediate threat. That arises because of the "new" drain on resources that is usually coupled to reduced economic prowess—often that two-pronged effect simultaneously accompanies Change. The reality is that Change demands a cost. For an organization, this cost can represent a heavy demand on cash flow and human resources. Therefore, successful Change is more likely to be effected when a firm has the resources, vitality, and know-how to implement and manage the required Change. It is only through a relationship framework that socioeconomic Change is conducted, managed, and processed. Thus, Relationship Theory gives us a model with which to better understand the "how's" and "why's" of Change as an operational dynamic. In summary, we know that

- Change is a key driver in society, in that it operates as a function of the relationship between the Life Cycle Dynamic's need for regenerative action and the consequent reaction.
- the relationship mechanism is humanity's adaptive response to the change pressure and challenge that the Life Cycle Dynamic causes.
- society itself provides both the framework and the opportunity for relationship entities to perform in the world and to gain access to the resources required to satisfy their goals.

RELATIONSHIP DYNAMICS

- in forming relationships we create an interactive matrix of elements that together identify the manner in which we interact, and that give definition and structure to our society; aggregated, those component elements become the "fabric" of society.

CHAPTER 4

POWER AND CHANGE

POWER: A PRODUCT OF RELATIONSHIPS

In the last chapter we saw how and why change derives from the Life Cycle process of regenerative action and consequent reaction. In this chapter we will expand our analysis by looking at the concept of power and sanction. To move forward without the appreciation that that analysis will yield would be to neglect an intrinsic relationship within the architecture of societal living and an essential element of socioeconomic activity.

At this stage it is relevant to introduce a definition of Power. Of the many component requirements for successful life management strategies, the power constituent is a key conceptual device, as it lends much to the understanding of human activity. The definition of Power is based on

- analytical observation and experience.
- an appreciation that Power is an operational dynamic.
- the view that Power is a derived product of the relationship mechanism.

- the view that the reality of limited resources leads to the need for Power.

Therefore, Power is defined as *"the quality that results from the formation and operation of relationships, which gives an individual or group the ability to initiate, manage, direct, control, and/or resist, the process of Change."*

It is interesting to note that power has not been defined in terms of physical force. Power may be a physical or psychological force. The power invested in a relationship is combined with the dexterity of the entity in executing and managing that power. This represents a differentiating ability, one that is a key factor in the integrity of a relationship.

Society's ability to respond *differentially* is an important quality that the relationship mechanism bestows. That quality enables options to exist that have escalating degrees of consequence associated to them. In other words, it gives society an essential form of *choice*. That is an important ability because it also enables society to discard, avoid, and/or ameliorate, by and large, the potentially destructive applications of power that brute physical force can easily become.

Why must power exist? Because it is intrinsic to the nature of life. There are some simple realities that either our material wealth or our political affiliations may sometimes cause us to overlook.

- Life is a competitive process, in that resources are limited but demands are not.
- Relationships are the instrumental framework and mechanism that we employ to manage the competitive environment in which we exist.
- The ability to develop and apply appropriate applications

of Power is essential within any competitive environment that has limited resources.

Relationship Theory's fourth primary tenet states: *The social, economic, and physical pressures caused by the Life Cycle Dynamic result from the continual need for regenerative action and consequent reaction. In other words, engagement of the Life Cycle Dynamic's competitive challenge is responsible for the "change pressures" that affect our physical, social, and economic systems.*

Not only does that statement give the defining quality of change but it also depicts the functional process needed for the creation and management of power. The life force requires continual revitalization. For all forms of human association, especially business, the revitalizing process is about maintaining our vigor. Instrumental to that are the relationships that we form, change, and manage in order to effect the attendant and required power applications. In turn, the revitalized and vigorous forms will have been successfully created through and as a function of the relationship models that enabled the required resources to be supplied and managed appropriately.

The need for life to perpetuate itself causes it to drive its way onward as best it can. Though much of our social and political debate does not truly embrace the competitive reality of our existence, it should never be forgotten that the very act of living is a competitive process, driven by the reality of excess demand for limited resources. Nowhere is that fact so keenly appreciated as in today's business environment. Whatever our desires and needs, their satisfaction will always require an engagement of relationships as the operational mechanisms through which the relevant but limited resources are to be obtained, managed, and delivered.

Therefore, any and every social construct gains its operational functionality through a balance of elements that determine its form. Likewise, the power applications generated are derived through that balance—one that represents a tension between rigidity and flexibility. Thus, our adaptive ability is a complex function that enables us to both determine and meet the need to reform so that power can remain appropriately applied.

Our adaptive response ability has developed to meet the demands and character of change. Society must have a vigorous but controlled response capacity. That capacity is assessed in terms of the scope and degree of our ability to react through the formation and reformation of sustainable and appropriate relationships.

Thus, society has a dynamic ability that is crucial for its integrity. If a society loses that prowess, its ability to hold together will become compromised at some point and, as a consequence, its social structure will no longer be viable. Therefore, a vital association is one that can appropriately apply Power and so achieve its global need to perpetuate itself, as well as all the situationally specific demands along the way.

Too great a rigidity may disable a society's ability to develop and execute adaptive responses. That becomes a probability when existing power models begin to "solidify" or are based on highly inflexible political or social constructs. Such models tend to resist and deny all forms of change. In effect, their "change strategy" is based on unqualified resistance. In turn, that creates the risk of developing the power model into a pathological, unsustainable construct—often a violent one.

Inflexible relationship models traditionally employ resistance as their form of change strategy. It is a strategy that can permeate every level of social endeavor with devastating effects—look at what happened to the Soviet Union. Its prescriptive socialist structure resisted change to the point where that country's industrial and economic organizations and body politic became fatally compromised. It will be interesting to follow the course of those same forms of interactive pressures within Communist China, because Chinese society has actually shown great aptitude, over the centuries, for using selective resistance as an effective strategy to manage social change.

The ability to form relationships is crucial for mankind's survival. It is that ability that enables us to create and apply power, with reference and in response to the consequential process of change.

THE EFFECTS OF CHANGE

Power has been identified as a requirement that arises as a result of limited resources. For us, it is also a relationship product that is intrinsic to the *process of consequent change*. In other words, *power* is not some discrete entity/ability that stands alone and is "there" as power in itself. Power is a function of the relationship mechanism and is applied with reference to Change and the adaptive responses that individuals or groups formulate to effect Change.

Change will always cause some form of reactive response. Indeed, that is required. However, the problem lies not in the fact that there is reaction but in ensuring that the content, direction, and manner of that reactive response is appropriate and effective.

Sustained success relies on strategies that meet the challenge of Change and the need for stability—in such a way that the ability to continually apply and reapply appropriate applications of power without losing organizational cohesion is never compromised. This is a key characteristic of any successful business.

As life is a dynamic process, it requires that its propagators have an ability to make adaptive responses. Therefore the dynamism of life will involve and necessitate movement. New and different directions of movement will translate as change adjustments.

Western society has made many significant and successful "change adjustments" over the last four centuries of its social and economic development. It has done so in the face of huge social, political, and economic demands. During that period Western society moved its principal focus from agrarian operations to manufacturing and on to information and systems. Significantly, this was achieved without losing the ability to manage the necessary requirements of being able to feed, house, and defend its populations. Essentially, Western society has been able to maintain and apply effective power applications (adaptive responses) at all the crucial levels of demand throughout that vast program of change management.

For example, Western society successfully managed a complex array of change programs during the seventeenth and eighteenth centuries. During that period, the challenge concerned agrarian improvements and the development of our food-producing prowess. That program was often harsh and involved massive population movements from the country to the towns. It also placed a heavy demand for new technology and social organization. Then, during the eighteenth and nineteenth centuries, Western society focused on the development and expansion of its industrial and manufacturing base. The twentieth century was a very stressful period with huge global war costs—costs that underpin many of the structural and economic challenges we now face. That period also saw the development of large static corporations. From 1970 onward, the focus has been on information systems and flexible organizational environments that can rapidly respond to different change demands.

However, with all the criticism that is leveled at Western society, the immensity of its sustained management effort and achievement has become clouded. The fact that Western society managed a change program over four centuries without losing its ability to sustain its agrarian and manufacturing requirements is fantastic. The Soviet Union struggled to do that throughout its existence and fell apart within a fifth of that time.

Rarely throughout a prolonged period of accelerating development did Western society suffer a diminishing socioeconomic prowess or fail to improve the overall power and well-being of its populations in terms of absolute levels and thresholds of wealth, poverty, and socioeconomic prowess. The only exception was at the point of Change, such as the start of the Industrial Revolution. However, the social fabric soon adjusted to the new dependencies it had created with the development of new social-support structures, such as laws regulating work hours and working conditions.

It is important to note that Western society's economic growth and increased technical prowess were a function of its ability to improve the conditions promoting successful relationship formation. Success was not based on the primacy of the individual but on the ease and range of opportunities for individuals to enter into relationships that could result in appropriate power applications being devised to overcome the challenges of that time.

Earlier, under the section that dealt with Individuality, it was found that Western society benefited from a more effective development strategy. This referred to a form of guidance and homeostasis that gave Western society a competitive edge in the creation of an environment where positive association was promoted. Therefore let's look briefly at how that guidance and homeostasis underpinned the historical events that unfolded.

Until the seventeenth century, Western societies were held rigidly in place by a range of legal and religious sanctions and beliefs. There were highly prescriptive and ordered political and social structures. As new ideas developed they were subject to tremendous resistance and persecution, often by the religious authorities of the day. However, as those respective changes matured, less violence and more ordered action returned to society. But it did so within a new environment. Within this new environment the essential need for structure and order, which had formerly been achieved by the previous highly prescriptive and regulated feudal system, was achieved largely by individuals who, though less regulated by external means, operated within strongly held social conventions. Those "internalized" conventions contained and accepted many of the requirements that the previous legal and religious sanctions had in part promoted, such as a sense of community, responsibility, and wider social service.

Thus, Western society's greatest industrial prowess was achieved within a framework of greater social mobility, which harnessed the strength of individuals who had generally a sense of faith, responsibility, and duty; an appreciation of community; a sense of contribution; and a notion of exchange which accepted that reward had to be earned. Those were critical elements of many of the relationships that were formed during that time.

Western society's new relationship environment had far fewer social "policing" costs than the old one; that accelerated the promotion of relationships yielding greater overall wealth. In turn, that wealth and economic power facilitated and enabled welfare legislation—from the Poor Laws of Tudor England to the formation of universal national health services in all the developed countries except Switzerland and the United States.

Thus, Western society's more competitive and less costly relationship model enabled it to gain and sustain an advantage throughout the last four hundred years of its exploration, colonization, and agrarian and industrial revolutions. During that period, compared to the highly regulated and rigid societies of the East, Western society's relationship model became increasingly more flexible, especially as regards successive Western societies' abilities to take "the mantle of leadership." While one country's economic prowess failed, another reformed, developing more effective and competitive relationship models.

The economic rise of Great Britain, France, and Germany, followed by that of the United States of America, was possible because those societies were better able to mobilize their populations into more effective relationship models— which, in turn, enabled the talents of individuals to rise to the fore. It must be remembered that within any successful society, its power applications are being continually and appropriately applied, reapplied, and reformatted.

RELATIONSHIP DYNAMICS

Today, Western society has two primary challenges. One challenge is posed by the development of an information-based society and the increasing drive for Change caused by our ability to transmit information faster and more effectively. Meanwhile, there is an underlying challenge posed by an apparent change in the character of the internalized conventions of its populations. The questions that arise from these challenges are the following.

- What does it mean for our society today if we no longer have a fundamental sense of faith, responsibility, duty; an appreciation of community; a sense of contribution; or a notion of exchange which accepts that reward has to be earned?

- If we now move toward a rights and legalistic basis for relationship formation and association, as offered by the politically correct agendas, does that mean that we are introducing ever higher association, policing, and operational costs—costs that will accelerate our lack of competitiveness?

- Do individuals in Western society now enter into relationships with a fundamental sense that reward is based on a a "right" that "falls due"?

- Is consumption now based on a concept that one has a "right" to self-gratification, regardless of the consequences to others?

If the answers to the above are "Yes," then in seeking to meet the need to successfully revitalize and regenerate, Western society will have an increasingly difficult task. Therefore, not only will our competitive ability against all comers become eroded, but so too will our ability to maintain our operational *baseline needs*.

THE MANAGEMENT OF POWER

The need to maintain a vital and successful response ability means that we have to be able to promote the formation of relationships which, in turn, will generate the appropriate power applications. Thus, power is multiaspected and from its definition, involves

- management, direction, control, and resistance of the cause-and-effect process of change.
- a variety of other elements that surround those multidimensional aspects; critical elements relate to knowledge, capability, access to resources, and effective strategy selection.

All those aspects are operated and controlled within and through the relationship mechanism.

The definition of Power, its multiaspected guises and its active reference to the process of change, is a further reason for us to study and appreciate the value of Relationship Theory. Why should this be? Consider what is being suggested.

- That mankind's adaptive ability is manifested and delivered through relationships.
- To promote that adaptive ability, we have evolved within a structure we call society.
- Society is defined by and composed of the aggregated character and number of its relationships sets.
- Successful life adaptations represent successful power applications.
- Social, economic, political, and military power are functions and abilities that result from the Relationship mechanism.

- The Life Cycle Dynamic is characterized by the need to continually revitalize.
- Revitalization introduces variation, which is identified and corresponds to the reactive Change adjustments that are being made.
- Successful societies are those that are able to make effective and appropriate change adjustments.
- Every change adjustment represents an adaptive relationship response that is made in order for an appropriate power application to be applied or reapplied.

All of the above result from the operation of society's relationship mechanism. Additionally, we should all appreciate the most extreme effects of possible Power applications, especially inappropriate ones, which can lead to pathological Power models. It should be noted that pathological Power applications are more likely to be generated when there is a predisposition to focus on the Control and Structure dimensions of relationships. A good example of this is represented by the organizational structures built by totalitarian states and, of late, those proposed by its modern-day version, "political correctness."

Much has recently been written about diversity and its place in improving the performance of organizations. Diversity and variation, of themselves, do not necessarily give one a competitive advantage, nor are they performance statements. Any CEO who says, "We have a very diverse workforce" is not actually saying that the company is therefore a better or more competitive one. That statement simply means that great differences exist within the organization.

Indeed, a competitive advantage is not about promoting diversity but has to do with the wielding of the resources you have available, however diverse and varied they are, into an appropriate, effective, and successful response to whatever challenge has been made. To underline that point, Japan, compared to the United States, has a very homogeneous society and little ethnic or racial diversity but is highly competitive and successful.

Therefore, it is also important that we learn the limitations of the social structures that we build and the extent of our varied expectations of them. Expectations arise in every situation and are integral to all empowerment processes. However, none of that understanding will be possible without a detailed study of the relationship mechanism.

SANCTION

Sanction closely follows on from the concept of power. The term *sanction*, as opposed to *coercion, penalty,* or *force,* is used here because it offers us greater scope in the identification of the various devices, ploys, and guises to do with sanction engagement. Also, coercion, penalty, and force tend to be associated with naked and overtly aggressive actions involving threat, physical violence, or specific violations against one party by another. Further, those terms seem to be aligned with non-legal and/or criminal formats of application. Therefore, Sanction is concerned with all of the above plus the less discernible and somewhat amorphous nature of many of the devices that are used to impel or "force" an abnormal or irregular effect upon the entities in a relationship.

Within relationships a multiplicity of tactics and strategies can be used by one entity to compel a relationship to be formed, sustained, controlled, changed, and operated with another entity who would never be party to the relationship otherwise. Thus, there is also an underlying directionality and sense of magnitude to *Sanction* in terms of the respective entities' relationship "weight." Sanction plays a dual role in the relationship mechanism, in that

- it sits intrinsically around and within the four dimensions that constitute the formation and operation of relationships, and
- it is also a consequence that is engaged as a global discipline concerning the function of life—i.e., it underscores the operation of that dynamic function.

We will look at the latter facet of Sanction first. Most of us unconsciously know the range of "sanctions" that could limit the operation of our everyday lives. That knowledge stresses an essential quality that is an integral function of the Life Cycle Dynamic: if the Life Cycle Dynamic loses its ability to revitalize and remain vital, then the ultimate Sanction is confronted; the final consequence for animate beings comes into play—life ceases.

We are all governed by that bottom-line Sanction. Working up from there, every revitalization exercise and process carries with it an implicit Sanction. In our lives we are subject to a variety of Sanctions. The following are examples of the "global" sanctions of discipline.

- *Legal:* break the law and penal Sanctions apply.
- *Regulatory:* break the rules and get thrown out of the game.
- *Commercial:* fail to meet your customers' needs and your margin of profit shrinks.

- *Social:* "legal" but inappropriate behavior will not get you into trouble with the law, but it will probably severely limit your social access, opportunities for interaction, and development.
- *Intersocietal:* potentially cataclysmic as the Sanctions can range from diplomatic, legal, and financial exercises to all-out war. It is significant that all of these manifestations are deemed "legal" provided they correspond to an accepted format, such as a "declaration of war" by one state against another.

All the above are examples of the global Sanctions that apply within and around the competitive demands that face society. Those types of Sanctions are very much operational disciplines and they are both a consequence and a relationship derivative—the latter in that they arise as a result of forming or failing to form an effective relationship. Also, at a "global" level, those Sanctions underpin the formation and operation of all our relationships.

Sanction comes into play in relationships either as a limited form of control mechanism or as a direct force when the basis of the relationship is disputed. *Sanction involves the ability of one entity to apply or threaten to apply some form of negative consequence upon another entity if the latter does not acquiesce.* That threat, or resulting action, may include both legal and nonlegal systems of organized force. It would also include pathological manifestations, whether they be initiated by military, political, or criminal groups. Sanction is often applied incrementally and can therefore be used as an early warning indicator of the viability and quality of a current organization's relationship model.

CHAPTER 5

THE STRUCTURE
OF RELATIONSHIPS

Relationship Dynamics identifies the structure of relationships and the mechanisms through which they operate. The
message is powerful and the impact direct—once seen, you
can never unsee it. It identifies the need to make a dimen-

Figure 5.1
The dimensional shift

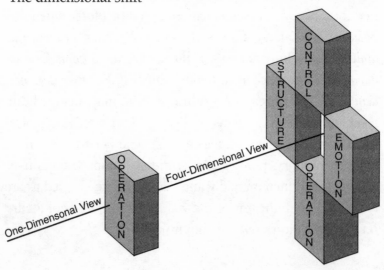

sional shift in the way we see situations. To fully understand the operation of relationships we must move from a one-dimensional view, focused only on the operation dimension, to a four-dimensional view focusing on

- control
- emotion
- operation
- structure

RELATIONSHIP INTERACTIONS

As stated on page 29 in Chapter 2 on the Motivational Basis of Relationships, the internalized dimension of individuals defies deconstruction. Therefore within Relationship Dynamics we accept that relationship understanding must come from an analysis of the interaction between the parties to a relationship. Thus, when attempting to understand a relationship, the starting point can be either an overall perception or a more detailed understanding of each specific relationship interaction. The understanding generated from either view will usually determine whether there is a need for analysis from the other perspective as well. For example, the relationship between a manager and his employees may involve many specific types of interaction, such as

- job instruction
- performance evaluation
- training
- informal discussion
- specific assistance with tasks
- social interaction (which may itself consist of many interaction subtypes)

Each of these interaction types has a specific relationship profile that relates to its specific situation. The overall view of the relationship may have a profile that is in line with the view of each specific interaction or it may be somewhat different. This is possible because there can be a qualitative difference in the nature of specific and general relationships and the manner in which they are perceived. Thus, relationships must be understood on the basis of their context and different perceptions can quite correctly exist about what appear to be the same situations.

This intertwining of the effects of interactions between people at various levels is what makes the understanding and management of relationships so successful. Relationship Dynamics provides a basis for unraveling those effects, identifying their source, and then addressing them in a controlled and systematic fashion.

THE COMPONENTS OF RELATIONSHIPS

Relationships can be usefully viewed on two different levels. The high-level perspective enables an overall perception to be generated and an intuitive understanding to be developed. The detailed-level perspective enables a relationship to be evaluated in depth and provides individual performance profiles that can be monitored within groups and over time.

At a high level, information can be gathered that provides an initial understanding of the manner in which a relationship operates. This high-level view of relationships involves

- identifying the entities involved in the relationship
- alignment: the respective entities' goals, roles, and scope

- assessing the relative weight, flexibility, and direction of a relationship
- noting all parties' perceptions of the relationship's optionality, importance, viability, and effectiveness

THE ENTITIES INVOLVED IN A RELATIONSHIP

The entities in a relationship will be either individual or aggregated and can be of many types, such as

- individual people
- groups of people, such as teams, organizations, countries, etc.
- other entities such as animals, resources, or products (For example, many people would claim to have a relationship with their car.)

An entity can also be viewed either as an instance or as part of a type. For example, the set of managers who conform to a management type involve many different in-

Figure 5.2
Relationship views

Relationships can be viewed at two different levels.

A high-level view that identifies the
outcome of a relationship

A detailed-level view that identifies the
internal operation of a relationship

Broad External Perspective

Detailed Internal Perspective

stances of Manager. An individual manager is an instance of the type Manager. In any situation a relationship may be viewed from the perspective of an individual instance, i.e., a specific manager, or from the perspective of the type Manager, which may include many actual managers. It is important to identify the best perspective from which to understand a relationship, because the relationship may operate in a different manner for each different entity-type view involved.

For example, we can evaluate the relationship between a customer and the product he buys from the sales representative of a specific company. The customer may perceive his relationship with the product to be different from his relationship to the salesman and his relationship to the company. He may approve of the product, but not the company or the salesman. He may trust the salesman, but not the company. He may respect the company, but not the particular salesman. Or he may distrust the salesman type in general, but trust this specific salesman. This myriad of possible

Figure 5.3
The high-level components of relationships

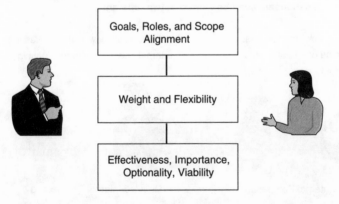

relationship interactions makes it important to have a clear understanding of relationships and the way entities operate within them.

ALIGNMENT: GOALS, ROLES, AND SCOPE

Alignment is a theoretical construct that Relationship Dynamics uses to describe the degree of correspondence that exists between the parties to a relationship. We form relationships because we need and or want to achieve desired outcomes. That is, relationships are normally formed for a purpose, and successful operation is largely dependent upon the degree of correspondence or similarity between the respective entities. The appropriateness of a relationship, its effectiveness, as well as the overall and individual success of the entities involved, are greatly influenced by the degree of relationship alignment.

Therefore the goals, roles, and scope of operation of the entities in a relationship define the context, nature, and direction of the relationship. Many relationships run into problems at this level. Where these elements are not clearly understood by both entities, the potential for problems is massive.

Often a simple focus on the appropriate goals, roles, and scope can resolve seemingly impossible relationship problems. Each entity in a relationship has come to the relationship with a goal to be achieved. This goal may be complex, such as to develop a long-term personal relationship, or simple, such as to execute a small transaction to buy a product. Many relationships generate problems because the goal of each participant is not clearly understood by the other and/or compatible with the goals of the other.

Figure 5.4
Role alignment

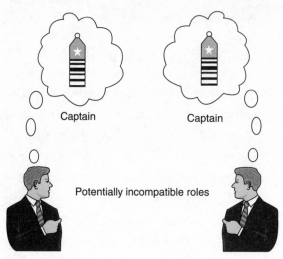

Figure 5.5
Incompatible goals

Figure 5.6
Scope alignment

Each entity performs one or more roles in a relationship. The roles performed provide a specific context for that entity within that relationship. This context has a major impact on the manner in which the entities interact in the relationship. Where entities take on inappropriate roles, they will often find it harder to achieve their goals.

Each relationship operates within a particular environment. For example, it would normally be seen as inappropriate for your manager at work to start attempting to apply his authority gained in the work environment to your personal relationships. Where this occurs there are often major problems. The scope of the workplace relationship does not normally include the home life of the parties to it.

WEIGHT, FLEXIBILITY, AND DIRECTION

At the high level, a relationship can be thought of as having the properties of weight, flexibility, and direction. These capture the essence of the relative influence of each party to a relationship.

Weight refers to the level of influence that one party has over the other party in the relationship. This influence reflects the ease with which an entity can initiate or resist change in the relationship. Weight arises as a function of a relationship's composition, i.e., both the relationship dimensions, with their elements, impart an intrinsic weight to each entity who is party to the relationship. For example, one party may enjoy a tremendous influence over the other as a result of heavy emotional investment, e.g., the other party loves him and will do anything to keep the relationship going.

Flexibility is another "imparted" quality that arises out of a relationship's specific composition and its situational framework. In other words, the dimensions of the relationship, and the specific elements by which the association is driven, greatly affect how much flexibility that relationship will have. Simply, *flexibility* refers to the ease with which the relationship can adjust as the relationship changes or the relative weight of the entities changes. Therefore, a flexible relationship is one that can adjust easily to such change— an inflexible relationship does not respond well to change and may well fracture completely.

Direction refers to the principal driver that causes a relationship to form and upon which subsequent interaction is based. Direction will also identify which entity it is that drives the relationship. The direction will depend on the nature of the relationship. A partnership is likely to have a bidirectional or two-way basis, whereby both entities agree on the nature of the relationship, whereas a bureaucratic relationship is likely to have a unidirectional or one-way basis, whereby the entity representing the bureaucracy defines the nature of the relationship. (This concept of specific relationship styles is developed in the following chapters.)

An awareness of these high-level elements of a relationship enables a powerful understanding of its likely underlying dynamics. These concepts can be brought together to create a view of the overall structure and dynamic operation of a relationship. Taking two ends of the spectrum as examples, we can identify the likely nature of a balanced and flexible relationship and of a rigid and skewed relationship.

A balanced and flexible relationship will tend to be

- operated with appropriate direction
- self-regulating
- easily negotiated
- less formally organized
- intrinsically understood
- proactive
- jointly and equally empowered

A rigid and skewed relationship will tend to have

- a strong directional bias
- formal or legal sanctions behind it
- barriers to negotiation
- a defined and fixed negotiation ritual
- much formality
- often become esoteric
- a reactive style

A balanced and flexible relationship is not necessarily better than a rigid and skewed one; it depends on the circumstances. For example, the standard model within the armed forces is a rigid and skewed one; there is a nonnegotiable, formal, and unidirectional relationship between those in command and those subject to command. The aim is to generate a body of men and women who can respond to high-level decisions immediately and without question.

In commercial life, the traditional corporate organization had a similar relationship orientation, to enable it to benefit from economies of scale and hierarchically defined action. As organizations have had to respond in a faster, more flexible manner this basic relationship model has begun to change. Control structures have opened up, and decision making and action are being devolved to those who actually carry out tasks.

By creating this overall picture of the weight, flexibility, and direction of a relationship it is often possible to identify the strategic problems within an organization in terms of its basic mode of operation and its cultural influence on its members.

OTHER HIGH-LEVEL CONCEPTS

At this high level, general impressions are created about a relationship. These impressions are generated by the general performance of the relationship and can be identified by the following concepts:

- optionality
- importance
- viability
- effectiveness

The perception of these aspects by each party affects the manner in which the relationship operates. Each entity can either choose to enter into a relationship or find that the situation he is in forces him into a relationship. This initial formation of a relationship can affect its operation. There is no guarantee that an optional relationship will be better than a mandatory one, but the influence of the formation of the relationship should be considered when its performance is being investigated.

The relative importance of a relationship to each party will have an effect on the relationship. Again there is no fixed rule about the influence of importance, except that where the parties ascribe different levels of importance to the relationship there is the potential for problems and misunderstanding. The long-term viability of the relationship reflects each party's view of the sustainability of the relationship under a particular set of conditions. *Viability* includes the attainment of a sustainable desired outcome, rather than just the effectiveness of the relationship. The *effectiveness of a relationship* is the ability of that relationship to generate the specified outcome. The outcome can be created, but may not be sustainable.

The high-level view provides the basis for an evaluation of relationship performance without the need to look in depth at the performance of each entity involved in the relationship. This view enables a judgment to be made about the overall alignment and operation of a relationship.

Where this overall view is favorable and those involved in a relationship believe that it is operating well, that relationship can be seen as operating in an appropriate manner. Where the overall view is not favorable and there is a problem in a relationship, the resolution may well lie in adjusting its goals, roles, or scope and the other high-level influences. This enables relationship problems to be quickly identified at an external, "objective" level and then addressed without the need to investigate the detailed performance of the parties to the relationship.

Where the overall view is favorable but there is a problem in a relationship, this indicates that the relationship is in alignment in terms of its objectives, but there is a problem in the way the parties are performing. The detailed performance of each entity must therefore be investigated in order to understand and address the problems.

THE DETAILED-LEVEL VIEW

At a more detailed level, relationships involve four dimensions and many elements that work in concert to generate the overall impressions we develop. Each of the different dimensional elements contributes to this overall relationship matrix, both singly and interactively. In many situations, people find it difficult to consider and react to the uncovering of these more detailed aspects because they have no structure to help organize and understand them. Relationship Dynamics provides a simple but powerful definition of these elements and their interaction. The detail level aspects can be identified at the two sublevels of dimensions and elements.

DIMENSIONS AND ELEMENTS

The relationship framework is defined in terms of its component *dimensions*. We have identified four dimensions of relationships that capture the essence of relationships (see Figure 1.1), namely

- control
- emotion
- operation
- structure

Emotion and operation have fundamental properties that are evaluated in absolute terms. *Absolute evaluation* means that the higher the value ascribed to them, the more effective the relationship. For example, a high level of acceptance and approval will always indicate a more effective relationship than a low level of acceptance and approval.

Control and structure are situationally specific dimensions. They have fundamental properties that are evaluated

Figure 5.7
Relationship dimensions and elements

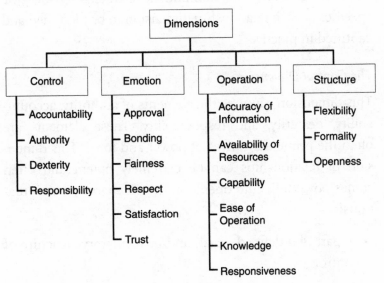

only in relative terms. *Relative evaluation* means that the value ascribed to them only has meaning in terms of the situation within which the specific relationship finds itself.

For example, a high level of control ascribed to one of the entities in a relationship may be good or bad, depending on the nature of that specific relationship. It may be that to achieve the desired outcome one entity *needs* to control the relationship; in that case a high control value would be appropriate. If, however, the relationship requires a balanced, shared level of control, then a high ascribed value for one entity would indicate problems for the relationship and the goal it exists to achieve. Situationally specific evaluation revolves around the variation between the dimension profiles that would support effective operation of the relationship and the values actually ascribed to the parties to the relationship.

Each relationship dimension comprises a number of component elements that define its character and that can be seen to have a major impact on the operation of relationships in general. The component elements enable the specifics of each relationship dimension to be identified and captured in practice.

The Control Dimension

This dimension captures the elements of authority, accountability, dexterity, and responsibility. These elements are often the prime derivatives of power and force. This dimension of relationships can be extremely potent and often comes powerfully into operation in two characteristic situations:

- as part of a defined, legal, and/or regulatory structure of control

- in response to failure in one of the other relationship dimensions

In the first situation identified above, if the structure of the relationship is ill defined, misunderstood, or not accepted, it is likely that there will be problems with the relationship, and challenges will occur. However, even successful applications of control can be problematic. The utilization of control elements to force a solution, rather than address the real issue of the other relationship dimensions, will always generate incomplete solutions. In some situations it will be necessary to apply increasing control, but this should only be done in full knowledge of the potential implications.

A good example of the control dimension in operation is the functioning of regulatory bodies. Many people have problems dealing with regulatory bodies. Likewise, regulatory bodies often find it difficult to improve the perception of their relationship with those they regulate. We have found that many of the regulatory bodies with whom we deal tend to manipulate the control dimension whenever a situation becomes difficult. Rather than evaluate an issue, understand the desired outcome, and look to improve the situation, the responses of regulatory bodies tend to revert to statements of force.

A typical ploy involves the manipulation of information. The best way for a regulatory body to make statements of force is to hide information showing whether or not that force is justified, fair, or reasonable. This tactic enables regulatory bodies to render many challenges by those regulated nearly impossible, because the justification for compliance or noncompliance is kept hidden.

RELATIONSHIP DYNAMICS

Unfortunately, this control tactic is natural for those who operate within a regulatory framework. Regulatory bodies are invested with the power to apply force and control in specific circumstances. Their function—to oversee the operation of individuals and groups in specific situations—is legal and proper. Therefore they will have a natural tendency to direct and enforce. There is, however, a balancing mechanism to this; it comprises the defined process of operation, the specific legislative mandate, and the principle of fair and reasonable action. Regulatory bodies must operate within the bounds set by these.

Successful management of regulatory relationships is promoted by confronting the control-dimension elements directly. This strategy enables and facilitates a change in the balance of control by making explicit the defined operational parameters that should be observed. Further, it is crucial to show how the relevant relationship dimensional elements are, and should be, interacting. This approach enables the nature of the relationship to become clear. Therefore, should control be inappropriately manipulated by one party to a relationship, then this manipulation, once demonstrated and made explicit, becomes obvious and ultimately untenable.

The control dimension can usefully be split into four specific elements that each have their own characteristics: authority, accountability, execution, and responsibility.

Accountability refers to the degree to which an entity can be called to account for the result of the relationship. Accountability should go hand in hand with authority and responsibility. Where accountability is divorced from responsibility and/or authority, the normal functioning of a relationship is likely to be compromised.

As organizations change and flatten their structures, and as more people work as independent agents, the accountability of individual action becomes more naked. In the past accountability was often lost within the labyrinthine structures of organizations. As the older-style organizations reform themselves into more direct and accountable formats, a major challenge will be to get those who previously avoided accountability to accept that they must become directly accountable for their actions.

Authority refers to the degree of control that an entity exercises over another entity. Authority is the empowerment that enables and sanctions an entity to initiate and direct action. This empowerment can be invested in the entity by society in general, by an organization, or by a group. It can also be generated through that entity taking physical power in opposition to the wishes of society or specific groups. The nature of authority, as well its degree, has an effect on the operation of a relationship.

Authority includes the notion of *justified power*. A person with authority usually has the legal right and responsibility to exert influence in certain situations. That person is also in some way accountable for action taken. Authority, responsibility, and accountability go hand in hand. However, there are many situations where people exercise authority without wishing to incur accountability. Authority without accountability is very dangerous because only the discipline of accountability allows control to operate on those with authority. This process is recognized in law by the general principle of "fair and reasonable" action. Within a relationship interaction there will be an appropriate division of authority, responsibility, and accountability that is dependent on the specific nature of the interaction. Where an authority profile is disputed or just inappropriate there will be problems in the relationship.

Dexterity is the ability of an entity to manage the relationship effectively. Knowledge of the expected and allowable modes of operation in any situation is important to the effective execution of control. Where the relationship is managed effectively, control tends to flow appropriately. Some individuals can manage relationships well, some may display an aptitude for some types of relationships, while others may be able to manage few elements of relationships successfully. Dextrous management of relationships is important because it can give one party a tremendous edge in the management of a relationship, whether or not that entity can perform effectively in delivering an effective operational outcome from the relationship.

It is important to realize that both situations and the social sanction for action can change over time. As a result, strategies that are appropriate for management at one point in time may become untenable at other times and in changing situations. This is why change can cause so many relationship problems. Change is problematic because it can cause people to lose sight of both the expected modes of operation and how they can be controlled.

Responsibility refers to the degree to which an entity takes on the duty to initiate and continue action. Responsibility must be compared to other component elements of the control dimension to discover how appropriate the allocation of responsibility is. In general terms, responsibility runs hand in hand with authority and accountability. In many relationship problems it is the lack of balance in taking on authority and accepting responsibility and accountability that causes the problem. The term *responsibility* has a specific dictionary definition that takes in two concepts: being held to account for taking action and being held to account for the result of action. *Responsibility,* as a term, has recently been used in situations that deny the accountability element. For this reason we have split the two concepts into the two elements of Responsibility and Accountability.

The Emotion Dimension

The first manifestation of relationship problems is often seen in the emotion dimension. When people begin to talk of dissatisfaction, unfairness, lack of trust, etc., this highlights emotional problems in a relationship. It is important to realize that, within the emotion dimension, responses are usually reactions to the outcomes generated from within the other dimensions. For example, the emotion of respect is usually created from generating effective and approved outcomes within the operation dimension.

Problems in the operation of a relationship, its control, or its structure often give rise to the feelings expressed within the emotion dimension. The most effective way to deal with the emotion elements of relationships is to manage the other dimensions successfully so as to generate a positive outcome.

Part of the authors' consultancy practice includes solution studies for relationships that have problems. Recently we dealt with a problem in the relationship between a regulatory body and a group of care-service providers. This relationship had begun amicably, and initially focused on the nature of the regulation process and specific operational issues. However, both of the entities were new to this particular combination of services and regulation. As a result, knowledge of the allowable regulation and the reality of operation was not fully or equally held on both sides. This led to problems in the relationship, whereby each side began to believe that the other was prosecuting its own particular agenda to the detriment of the first side. Quite soon the relationship became focused on personal issues, and a full-scale war developed, with each side accusing the other of lack of respect, trust, and fairness. Legal action was threatened by both sides and the relationship became untenable.

The nature of the interaction between the two sides had become skewed and misaligned. The interactions should have focused on the delivery of effective care to those in need. This changed into accusations arising from and affecting the emotion dimension—there was no longer approval, feelings of fairness, respect, or trust on either side. The consequence was that the prime operational relationship goal (to promote the development of effective services for those in need) became secondary.

The above profile of relationship development is not uncommon. When an operationally based relationship becomes solely fixed in the emotion dimension, it becomes unstable, volatile, and unable either to satisfy its goal or to generate the emotion of satisfaction for either entity. Satisfaction is usually attained as a result of successful operational outcomes, not direct manipulation of the emotion dimension. The misalignment between a direct focus on the emotional elements of a relationship and the need to generate successful emotional outcomes based on effective management of the other dimensions is at the heart of many relationship problems.

In our recent case we resolved the problem by working with both parties to help them focus back on the operational issues, which remained the initiating and prime reason for the formation of the relationship. In doing so, we did not deny the power of the emotion dimension; rather we helped the entities to appreciate that these powerful emotional issues were best addressed by repairing the relationship as a whole. We refocused them on the goals of the relationship, realigned their dimensional focus, and demonstrated that a degree of approval and fairness were necessary for the relationship to be able to work effectively for both sides.

A positive perception of the emotion dimension of a relationship determines that it is operating well. Emotion concepts such as happiness or love vary wildly among individuals and are not involved in every relationship, despite being very powerful drivers when they are present. Also they have very unpredictable results. Such deep-emotion concepts are often only understood by the individual experiencing them and are often not effective concepts to focus on in attempting to resolve the relationship problem. In evaluating and addressing relationship issues that are experiencing problems with those deep-emotion concepts, a focus on the elements we have identified here provides a "handle" that can be grasped to begin to identify and discuss what is happening in the relationship.

The emotion dimension can usefully be split into six specific elements that each have their own characteristics: approval, bonding, fairness, respect, satisfaction, and trust.

Approval refers to the degree to which an entity thinks that the participation of another entity is desirable. Relationships do not require approval to exist and operate effectively. Also, efficient and appropriate operation of the relationship does not require that approval be given equally by both entities. However, where there is *disapproval* by either entity, the effective operation of the relationship may become compromised. Therefore, an entity who does not approve of a relationship may still accept it and take part in it successfully, because they accept, for whatever reason, the overall need for the relationship, without approving of it.

Bonding refers to the degree to which an entity feels a strong sense of attachment to another entity in the relationship. This attachment can be based on other elements of the relationship or on just the emotional interaction between two entities. Emotion-based relationships can be highly volatile as they may have little ballast in the other dimensions to assist in the management of the relationship. Relationships based on bonding can therefore be both the most powerful and the most destructive of relationships.

Fair exchange refers to the degree to which an entity believes that the exchange that has occurred is fair. The concept of *fairness* means that the agreed basis of exchange results in both entities receiving something of an appropriate and acceptable value for their input. It does not mean receiving something in equal amounts. Effective, normally operated relationships usually include the concept of fair exchange. The basis of a "good deal" is that both entities feel and judge their own return as fair. In most Western societies, the concept of "fair and reasonable" is incorporated as a fundamental element in the legal system. Therefore whenever one or both of the entities in a relationship believe that the interaction is resulting in an outcome that is *not* fair and reasonable, this is likely to lead to problems and conflict.

Respect refers to the degree to which one entity values the participation and opinions of another. Respect is a relationship element derived from the effective operation of a relationship. The basic psychological need for respect, described previously as part of each individual's Critical Drive State, is a prime drive in individuals. Relationships that generate respect will be fundamentally much more effective than relationships which result in a loss of respect. The critical nature of this element is such that relationships that generate a loss of respect, esteem, and dignity are predisposed to violent reaction. The form of the violence may be self destructive, inward, or overtly revengeful.

Satisfaction refers to the degree to which an entity accepts and feels happy with the outcome of the relationship. Satisfaction is a general concept that is often used on its own in an attempt to understand the responses of people to situations. Within this context it provides an overall view of the entity's perception that can be compared and contrasted with the other elements.

Trust refers to the degree to which an entity believes that another operates in a fair and trustworthy manner. The level of trust in a relationship also has a major influence on the way the relationship operates. A high degree of trust facilitates operation of the relationship on an informal basis. If an informal operational climate is established, that will facilitate a relationship's capability to respond effectively to change. Trust will also tend to reduce the need to invest in rigid control structures. A low level of trust usually leads to the generation of rigid control processes, reduces the ability to generate appropriate responses to change, and uses up resources that could otherwise be used in improving the basic operation of this relationship or other relationships.

The Operation Dimension

The operation dimension's elements identify the overall ability to perform in a capable manner, i.e., the ability to achieve the required performance for the attainment of the defined goals. Within Relationship Dynamics, these elements provide an explanation about the operational characteristics of any situation. Obviously, any specific situation could involve a mass of detailed operational criteria that are specific to that situation. The component elements of operation deal with the simple need to have an effective and appropriate relationship. Relationships must have the power to perform. This power underlies, and can fundamentally impact across, all the relationship dimensions. Relationships that are well founded in the other dimensions can be compromised by the simple inability to perform appropriately.

Often operation problems are easy to identify. This ease, or obviousness, is often taken to mean that most relationship problems occur in this dimension. It should be noted, however, that operation is interactively associated with all the other relationship dimensions. This interactive nature means that problems in operation may be symptomatic of problems in the other relationship dimensions: "It isn't working well because they don't approve of the situation."

When people talk about inaccuracy, poor performance, or lack of response, they are usually referring to the inability of a relationship to achieve the required performance for the successful attainment of the relationship's goals. This dimension must operate effectively for any relationship to work well. Relationship Dynamics does not attempt to provide a basic structure for the almost infinite number of operational situations. Rather, it identifies key elements that capture the essence of good operation. Where operational problems are indicated, more detailed analytical techniques can be used to explore the specific nature of situations. Relationship Dynamics places the operation dimension within a wider context than just products and processes. This enables an understanding to be developed about all of the elements of a relationship.

The use of traditional approaches to problem solving, such as Total Quality Management, creates a focus on detailed operational issues of products and processes before any consideration is given to the other relationship dimensions. Relationship Dynamics captures the essence of effective operation much more quickly than Total Quality Management and enables an overall relationship view to be constructed. Where problems are identified in the operation dimension, then a combination of the directness of Relationship Dynamics and the greater detailed focus of existing approaches like Total Quality Management can be a powerful toolkit for their resolution.

Relationships that are more personal can also be aptly addressed through the operation dimension. Often personal problems result from an inability to perform within the operation dimension. However, personal problems are usually discovered first as impacting on the emotion dimension. Where operation problems are translated into emotion issues, resolution strategies can become difficult to identify or can be inappropriately applied. However, Relationship Dynamics provides a very powerful tool for identifying the underlying problem so that effective action can be taken to deal with the problem rather than merely dealing with the symptoms.

Most management approaches to problem solving are focused in the operation dimension, because this dimension provides the "hard" elements of products and processes. Products and processes are relatively easy to identify and quantify. Organizations tend to analyze problems within the operation dimension, such as the response time for customer requests or the number of defects per thousand of a production process. This approach generates information about the speed and scale of the response, not the quality and nature of the response. That information about speed of response is useful. However, if combined with information about the nature and impact of that response, it would provide a much more powerful understanding of the interaction.

The quantifiable nature of the hard elements promotes a tendency to restrict problem analysis to products and processes. However, Relationship Dynamics provides an analytical model that is able to identify and quantify both hard and soft elements. Therefore, Relationship Dynamics provides a wider perspective for the analysis of operational problems.

The component elements of the operation dimension comprise accuracy of information, availability of resources, capability, ease of operation, knowledge, and responsiveness, and capture the basic effectiveness of the relationship in operational terms. These are absolute elements, so the better they are, the better the overall relationship.

Accuracy of information refers to the degree of accuracy in the information provided by one entity to another. Successful operation requires that information be accurately passed between the respective entities within the relationship. Without accurate information, the raw material for developing effective strategies and appropriate tactical responses is severely limited. Information-based problems will have often unpredictable and probably negative consequences for a relationship.

Availability of resources refers to the degree to which resources are made available by an entity and are useful when required. Most effective relationships involve the sharing or exchange of resources. As organizations become flatter, with more focus on core competencies, the availability of appropriate resources becomes more critical. Control of resource availability facilitates the manipulation of a relationship. If either entity has a problem with the availability of resources, there are likely to be consequential relationship problems.

Capability refers to the general ability of an entity to carry out the tasks required by the relationship. As identified earlier, each relationship has a set of explicit or implicit goals within a scope of operation. Effective functioning for any relationship requires that each entity have the capability to work to achieve those goals.

Ease of operation refers to the degree to which an entity facilitates the ease of operation of the relationship. Ease of operation is a derived element. It captures the overall perception of an entity about the manner of operation. Easier operation is not necessarily better operation. Some situations will be intrinsically difficult. Therefore, it is important to analyze this element in terms of a specific situation.

Knowledge refers to the understanding that an entity has about the influences affecting a relationship. An entity can understand how to operate a relationship effectively but decide to use that knowledge to manipulate the relationship towards a preferred outcome. By looking at the knowledge an entity has, in combination with its ability to operate the relationship effectively, any such manipulation can be uncovered.

Responsiveness refers to the ease with which an entity adjusts in response to change in a relationship. The purpose of a relationship, expressed in its goal, scope, and role statement, defines or implies a level of responsiveness in the operation of the relationship. The importance of responsiveness depends on each specific situation. In some cases an inability to respond within a specific time may lead to the breakup of the relationship.

The Structure Dimension

We use the term *structure* to define the degree of flexibility, formality, and openness that operates in the relationship. Therefore, the structure dimension captures particular elements of the manner and style in which relationships operate. Relationships can and will operate with different degrees of flexibility, formality, or openness.

The structure profile identifies how a relationship will be able to select and apply its adaptive responses. Indeed, the way entities perceive and analyze problems will be greatly dependent on the way the relationship is operated.

For example, the flexibility, formality, or openness of the management will have a major impact on the effective performance of the relationships within an organization.

It must be remembered that all the dimensions of a relationship are interactive. As a result, it will often be the case that a structure profile must be as it is because it is critical for the effective operation of that particular relationship. It may also be that variation is just as allowable.

Organizations are faced with having to develop appropriate responses to various manifestations of change, such as the challenge of advancing technology, market demands for customized services, and cost model pressures. One characteristic way to improve the ability to generate fast and appropriate responses to those change pressures has been to reorganize, using a lighter/flatter management structure by removing whole layers of middle management. However, it was just those management layers that previously enabled the incremental definition and management of the operation of an organization. Effectively, little was invested in any single body or group of managers. Management was an aggregated effort.

Flatter management structures mean that organizations expect those who produce and/or deliver products and services to control their own work environment. Therefore, flatter management places greater responsibility on those remaining organizational levels; meanwhile there are fewer people responsible for management. This change in operation is seen as being most successfully accommodated by allowing individuals greater flexibility to operate. Flexibility exists as a component of the structure dimension within both formal and informal organizations. As layers of control and checking are removed, the processes within organizations become, by necessity, more open. As organizations have to work together, costly duplication in checking and control process can be avoided by opening up their processes to each other.

Each of the elements of the structure dimension is relative. There is no general level of performance that is better than any other. The specific situation determines the appropriate level of each structure element.

Flexibility refers to the capability of an entity to respond to change in the relationship. Flexibility is a key factor in the successful operation of a relationship in today's fast-changing world. People will require flexibility in the skills they develop, the tasks they are willing to take on, and the manner in which they operate in the world. As organizations focus more on the specific performance of individuals and teams, the requirement to respond flexibly increases.

Formality refers to the degree to which an entity enforces rigid rules or conventions in a relationship. Formality is not necessarily good or bad. Some situations will require formal structures and responses, while others will require informal ones. It is important not to use formality to generate control, especially where control is inappropriate.

Openness refers to the degree to which an entity has access to the processes, resources, decisions, and thoughts of the other entity in the relationship. The effective operation of many relationships requires that one entity be able to question the other and have access to answers and opportunities to reevaluate the relationship agenda.

THE OPERATIONAL FILTER

The *operational filter* (see Figure 5.8) is a key conceptual device that Relationship Theory employs within its motivational model. It has been included in this section of the book because of its particular utility for understanding the structure of relationships. Essentially, the operational filter illustrates and facilitates explanation concerning the predisposition that an entity will have towards the formation and operation of relationships. It is important for us to appreciate that each and every one of us has a predisposition that we take to every relationship and that its nature will affect the way that we seek, view, form, and operate relationships.

That predisposition will reflect and comprise elements from

- CDS in terms of the contribution that internalized drives

THE STRUCTURE OF RELATIONSHIPS

Figure 5.8
The operational filter

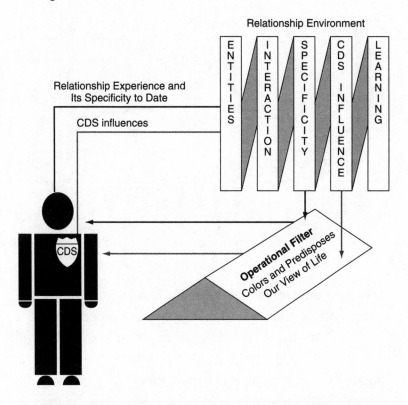

have as regards an individual's characteristic style of association.

- The experience and specificity to date of an entity's relationship formation and operation.
- The specificity that applies to the situations under which an entity has formed or seeks to form a relationship.

Everyone has an operational filter that colors his view of the world. That "coloring" represents the way in which we particularize information. Perceptions are built with refer-

Figure 5.9

Comparing the medical and care operational filters

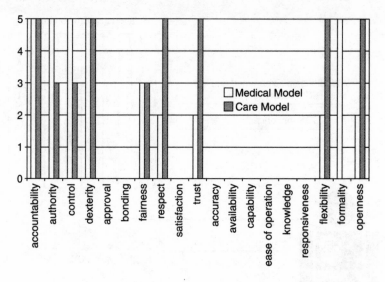

ence to our internalized meaning framework; simply, the cognizance of "data points" is a subjective process. Thus, it follows that ongoing relationship experience and CDS will further orient and contribute to the "refraction" effect of the operational filter vis-à-vis external interaction.

Figure 5.8 captures that last point as well as the interactive process that is at work. Importantly, it illustrates that relationship formation and operation is oriented, understood, and then built upon through a process in which the operational filter plays a fundamental role. That role means that

- the relationship entities that we seek to form relationships with,
- the character of the interaction that then develops,
- the specificity of the demands that then arise, and
- the internal needs and demands as represented by our CDS

are all constituent parts of an interactive process of learning upon which the operational filter exerts a crucial and necessary influence. The word "*necessary*" is used here because all life experience involves a subjective exercise of meaning and understanding. Therefore the operational filter itself is likely to become modified as our relationship experience and the specificity of our life needs develop over time.

Once understood, the concept of the operational filter enables us to develop and apply an essential element concerning the analysis and identification of relationship styles and types. Figure 5.9 shows a relationship profile of two different operational filters for the performance of a physician in a relationship with a patient. (The next chapter on Relationship Analysis explains the details of a relationship profile.)

The higher the score for each relationship element, the more of that element is found in the performance of the

Figure 5.10
The changes required by the physician to move to the care model

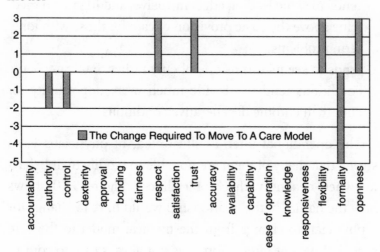

physician in the identified relationship. The information in the relationship profile table shows that the classic approach taken by the medical profession features a high degree of control, disempowerment of the patient, and the operation of a closed and esoteric process. This approach is sensible when there is an acute situation that requires immediate skilled action to preserve the life of a patient. But there has traditionally been a problem in the medical profession in that this relationship model has been applied to both acute situations and chronic situations which do not involve the need for immediate action. As a result of this predisposition of the medical operational filter, many people feel that physicians often treat them as objects rather than people.

The more normal predisposition to relationships between people in a non-life-threatening situation is one where control is shared and the interaction progresses on an open basis. This is reflected in the care operational filter profile shown in Figure 5.9. This inappropriate formation of relationships arises because the medical profession

- tends to value leading edge, intrusive, and high-tech medicine above the basic provision of care for those with long-term problems.
- tends to see its role as one of cure rather than care; acute conditions tend to provide much more opportunity for cure than chronic degenerative conditions.

The operational filter, as illustrated, of physicians is so strong that many of them are not able to modify their behavior when dealing with chronic illness. Figure 5.10 shows how the nature of the relationship would have to change for a physician to change from the medical model to the care model of patient interaction. It is not always easy to continually make such changes. This example shows how power-ful this predisposition is. By evaluating a relationship using Relationship Dynamics these issues become clear and can be shown to be in play. As a result the underlying influences at work in a relationship can be uncovered and steps put in place to address any issues found.

CHAPTER 6

ANALYZING RELATIONSHIPS

Relationship Dynamics provides an analytical process, called Relationship Analysis, that can be used to understand relationships in the real world. It identifies a series of simple but powerful steps that enable the behavior of relationships to be evaluated and understood. The process, as identified in this chapter, includes a series of basic steps. These basic steps can be applied in many different situations, but will usually involve the elements of scoping, alignment, and profiling, as identified below.

- *Relationship scoping:* this provides an overview of the entities and relationships involved in the issue being analyzed.
- *Relationship alignment:* this identifies issues that occur at the goal, role, and scope level. Where relationship issues are identified as those of alignment, they can often be addressed without the need to carry out a detailed analysis using relationship profiling.
- *Relationship profiling:* this addresses issues of detail in relationships.

Figure 6.1

Flowchart of the Relationship Analysis process

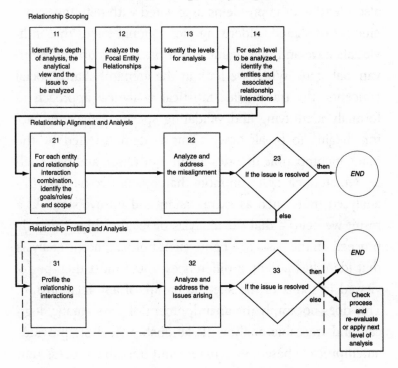

Each of these elements links seamlessly to the others. This integration supports both a top-down and a bottom-up approach to analysis. Relationship Analysis can be applied in either a systematic form, one that follows each step in detail, or a more general form that proceeds through each step but may not capture information in the same detailed and structured format. The more general approach is appropriate when analysis time is limited or those involved in the relationship are unlikely to provide detailed information.

It is important to understand the nature of the data collected by Relationship Analysis. In previous chapters we have talked about the concept of an open system that is not fully deterministic in operation and the need to look for general patterns of behavior rather than specific behaviors. We also identified the problems associated with defining a specific set of shared underlying motivational forces that individuals have and that defines their basic makeup and motivational state. When we look at the arena of shared social concepts, the traditional statistical analytical approach of formally identifying and validating specific behavioral factors begins to break down. This is demonstrated by the many incompatible theories about motivation and personality, which rarely agree on more than one or two basic factor-analyzed traits such as extraversion and introversion. As a result we believe that the analysis of relationships can only proceed on the basis of a lightweight nonparametric analysis that identifies potential differences; these must then be reviewed in terms of the specific nature of any relationship. This does not imply the abandonment of a systematic, logical, and traceable analysis. Relationship Analysis provides an empirically based, systematic, and traceable process that generates information about differences in the nature of perceptions about relationships. These differences can then be evaluated in terms of general rules and understanding of the social environment. The important issue is to have a traceable and systematic process that enables the evaluation to be understood and justified in any particular situation.

RELATIONSHIP SCOPING

Relationship Scoping identifies the environment within which the issue of concern operates. It comprises four steps:

- identification of the depth of analysis, the analytical view, and the issue to be analyzed

- analysis of the focal entity relationships, if strategic analysis is being undertaken
- identification of the level of analysis
- identification of the entities and their relationship interactions

Identification of the Depth of Analysis, the Analytical View, and the Issue to Be Analyzed

This step identifies the nature of the analysis to be undertaken. First, the depth of analysis is identified as either strategic or tactical. Strategic analysis provides an overview of a relationship in order to generate policies or plans of

Figure 6.2
Depth of analysis and analytical views

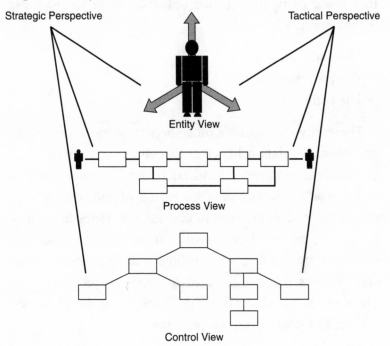

action associated with that relationship. Information is gathered about the entity types in a relationship to understand trends and medium to long-term issues. Tactical analysis provides a detailed view of a relationship in order to understand how specific outcomes are generated. Information is gathered about entity types and individual entities in specific situations. This distinction is important because the type of information gathered about a relationship will differ. Strategic analysis involves the collection of data about sets or populations of entity types while tactical analysis gathers information about the detailed operation of relationships. Often it will be appropriate to analyze a situation or issue from both the strategic and tactical perspectives.

While many different viewpoints can be taken, Relationship Analysis identifies three specific views of a situation that relate particularly to the operation of relationships in organizations.

- The entity view
- The process view
- The control view

The entity view focuses on a specific entity or entity type and all of the relationships that that entity or entity type has. The analysis is aimed at understanding how that entity or entity type operates and manages all of the relationships that it must form in order to address the issues being analyzed. The process view focuses on the specific process at issue; the entities and relationships analyzed form the roles and linkages that are required for the process to operate. The control view focuses on the lines of management and control in a team, group, or organization.

The issue to be analyzed is evaluated in terms of the depth of analysis and the view to be taken. It may be predefined in terms of a specific issue that has arisen, or an identified strategic goal. If Relationship Analysis is being carried out to uncover strategic options, then the second step in the scoping process, the generation of a focal entity relationship map such as Figure 6.3 will help to identify issues for analysis.

Focal Entity and Analyzing Focal Entity Relationships

The Focal Entity is the entity from whose point of orientation strategic examination is made. Plotting the focal entity's view creates the Focal Entity Relationship Map: a conceptual device that provides a representation of the essential relationship sets that the focal entity has identified as relevant. This is a high-level step that is useful in developing our strategic understanding as it provides an overview that quickly establishes a basic framework from which further analysis can be developed. The Focal Entity Relationship Map:

- identifies the main view of the issue that you wish to analyze
- links that main view to a specific entity: focal entity
- identifies the standard entity types with which the focal entity interacts
- identifies the main interaction between the focal entity and each relationship set/type

The map then provides a representation of the interaction between the focal entity and the entities with which the focal entity has formed relationships.

- Its relationship with regulatory or statutory bodies is characterized by compliance.

- Its relationship with customers is characterized by the satisfaction of need.
- Its relationship with suppliers is characterized by competitive supply.
- Its relationship with employees is characterized by endeavor, remuneration, and fulfillment.
- Its relationship with the funding source is characterized by viability.
- Its relationship with partners is characterized by shared goals.

To assist in understanding how Relationship Analysis operates we have included an example that runs through the rest of this chapter. The example involves a car dealership that is having problems in making retail sales of its top-of-the-line models. This is threatening the long-term profitability of the dealership. To understand these problems the dealership has performed a simple relationship analysis. The analysis will look at both strategic and tactical issues and be focused on a specific issue of "falling sales of top-of-the-line models."

The example in Figure 6.3 shows the Focal Entity Relationship Map for the initial analysis of the issue of "falling sales of top-of-the-line models." The car dealership is identified as the focal entity, that is, the entity from whose point of reference we wish to analyze the issue. The entities with whom the car dealership must form relationships are placed into the relationship type sections. For example, the relationship with the European Economic Community is identified as a regulatory relationship, the relationship with the car manufacturer as a supplier relationship, and the relationship with the purchaser as a customer relationship.

This representation of the basic entities involved and their

Figure 6.3
Focal Entity Relationship Map

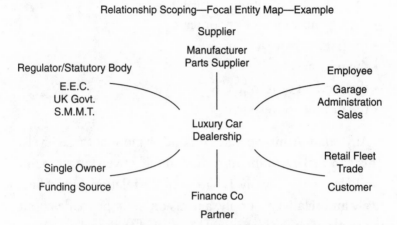

Relationship Scoping—Focal Entity Map—Example

Issue For Analysis: Falling Sales of Top-of-the-Line Models

relationships assists in identifying which relationships are most relevant to the issue of concern. In the example, the customer relationship is identified as the main one relating to the issue of falling sales. The regulatory, supplier, employee, partner, and funding-source relationships are identified as performing effectively and so will not be part of the initial analysis.

Identification of the Levels of Analysis

This step identifies the appropriate level of analysis for the issue(s) of concern. There are different levels of analysis possible for any relationship. For example, the relationship between a car salesman and a customer could be analyzed on the basis of car salesmen in general or a specific car salesman. There is a standard set of entity types that can be used to help structure the analysis of relationships in an effective manner. These types are

- the market type
- the market
- the organization, group, or team type
- the organization, group, or team
- the person type
- the person
- the product or resource type
- the product or resource

Any relationship operates on one or more of these levels. This can make it difficult to find an effective starting point for Relationship Analysis. To analyze relationships effectively and relatively simply, a decision must be made about the levels of analysis that will be applied to the relationship. In the example, the car dealership and the retail customer are dealt with as an organization and a person type respectively because there is one car dealership and many different customers.

Identification of the Relationship Interactions

This step identifies the entities involved and the Relationship Interactions that the relationships comprise. A Relationship Interaction Map is created for each relationship to be analyzed. The map includes the relationships involved in the issue of concern. For each relationship all of the relevant discrete Relationship Interactions are identified. The map is built up by identifying

- all of the entities that are involved in the issue of concern
- the set of Relationship Interactions that occur within those relationships

The example, reflected in Figure 6.4, shows that the issue

Figure 6.4

A Relationship Interaction Map

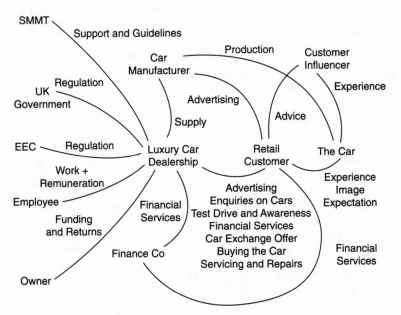

Issue for Analysis: Falling Sales of Top-of-the-Line Models

of concern, the falling sales of luxury cars, is affected by many entities. The sale of a car involves a whole series of separate relationship interactions, such as advertising, inquiries, and servicing and repairs.

The detail included on the Relationship Interaction Map will depend on the depth and level of both the analysis and the issue of concern. The example shows a relatively high-level description of each relationship interaction. These interactions could be broken down into more detailed discrete interactions. For example, the advertising relationship between the luxury car dealership and the customer may involve many specific interactions. A strategic analysis would start with the level of analysis used above; a more detailed tactical analysis might immediately look at each specific relationship interaction between the luxury car dealership and the customer. There is no hard-and-fast rule for the level of detail to be included on a Relationship Interaction Map. The process of analyzing the issue and drawing the map will usually direct the level of detail required in the analysis.

RELATIONSHIP ALIGNMENT

Relationship Alignment follows on from Relationship Scoping. It provides an analysis of the high-level operation of the relationships identified in Relationship Scoping. It comprises two steps:

- identification of the goals, roles, and scope of the entities in each Relationship Interaction
- analysis of Relationship Alignment

Identification of the Goals, Roles, and Scope of the Entities in Each Relationship Interaction

This step captures information about the nature of each relationship interaction. For each relationship, interaction information about the goals, roles, and scope of operation of both entities should be captured through an appropriate mechanism, such as structured questionnaires, general questioning, or observation. This information is used to document the goals that each entity is trying to achieve through the relationship interaction, the roles that each entity performs in the relationship interaction, and the scope of operation available to each entity in the relationship.

This information can be entered into a Relationship Interaction Alignment Table for future analysis (see Table 6.1). In the example an evaluation of the Relationship Interaction

TABLE 6.1

Relationship Interaction Alignment

Issue for Analysis	Falling sales of top-of-the-line models
Relationship Interaction	Servicing & repairs
Alignment of Goals, Roles, Scope	1 2 3 4 5
Flexibility	1 2 3 4 5

Entities	Luxury car dealership	Retail customer
Goals	To provide highly efficient and effective servicing and repairs with a minimum of disruption to the customer, and within the time and cost profile agreed	To receive an expertly serviced or repaired car within the time and cost profile agreed
	To make the customer feel delight at the service he receives	To receive treatment befitting a Luxury car customer
Roles	Mechanic	Customer
Scope	Within the agreed commercial terms and customer expectations	Within the agreed commercial terms and customer expectations
	Sales within the UK (and the EEC if requested)	
Weight	1 2 3 4 5	1 2 3 4 5
Optional/ Mandatory	Optional	Optional
Dynamic transaction role	Supplier	Customer
Importance	1 2 3 4 5	1 2 3 4 5
Viability	1 2 3 4 5	1 2 3 4 5
Effectiveness	1 2 3 4 5	1 2 3 4 5

Map and existing feedback from the retail customers identified that the main issue leading to falling sales is the performance of the dealership in providing effective servicing and repairs. Information has therefore been collected about this specific relationship.

Analysis of Relationship Alignment

This step identifies whether the issue of concern is addressed by the information gathered at this general level. If so, the analysis process is complete. If not, the more detailed level of analysis, called Relationship Profiling, is required. Information taken from the Relationship Interaction Alignment Table (see Table 6.1) is evaluated in terms of:

- the optionality of the relationship (it will be either optional or mandatory)
- the importance of the relationship
- the viability of the relationship
- the effectiveness of the relationship
- the alignment of the goals, roles, and scope of the entities in the relationship

This provides a high-level view of the relationship interaction and an indication of the likelihood of it performing in an effective manner. The assessment of importance, viability, effectiveness, and alignment can be scored on a simple 1 to 5 scale, with:

- 1 indicating a low level of the attribute
- 2 indicating a below average level of the attribute
- 3 indicating an average level of the attribute
- 4 indicating an above average level of the attribute
- 5 indicating a high level of the attribute

Where an issue or problem of concern is highlighted by this analysis step, action can be taken to start to address it. For example, if the goal of one entity was to promote an outcome that the other entity wished to stop, the goals would be out of alignment and the basis for the relationship might

TABLE 6.2

The Evaluated Relationship Alignment Table (evaluated scores are shown in bold face)

Issue for Analysis	Falling sales of top-of-the-line models
Relationship Interaction	Servicing & repairs
Alignment of Goals, Roles, Scope	1 2 3 4 **5**
Flexibility	1 2 3 4 5

Entities	Luxury car dealership	Retail customer
Goals	To provide highly efficient and effective servicing and repairs with a minimum of disruption to the customer, and within the time and cost profile agreed	To receive an expertly serviced or repaired car within the time and cost profile agreed
	To make the customer feel delight at the service he receives	To receive treatment befitting a Luxury car customer
Roles	Mechanic	Customer
Scope	Within the agreed commercial terms and customer expectations	Within the agreed commercial terms and customer expectations
	Sales within the UK (and the EEC if requested)	
Weight	1 **2** 3 4 5	1 2 3 4 **5**
Optional/ Mandatory	Optional	Optional
Dynamic transaction role	Supplier	Customer
Importance	1 2 3 4 **5**	1 2 3 4 **5**
Viability	1 **2** 3 4 5	1 2 3 **4** 5
Effectiveness	1 **2** 3 4 5	1 **2** 3 4 5

be brought into question. If the car dealership wished to provide a minimal level of service and customer interaction, that would be out of alignment with the goals of the customer. In the example Table 6.2 shows that the goals, roles, and scope of operation of the luxury car dealership and the retail customer are in alignment, but that effectiveness and viability of the relationship have not scored high in all cases. This indicates that the dealership and the customer agree on what the relationship should provide, but that in practice that outcome is not being created. Therefore, despite the goal, role, and scope being in alignment, there is a more detailed problem in this relationship that requires a detailed analysis through Relationship Profiling.

RELATIONSHIP PROFILING

Relationship Profiling follows on from Relationship Alignment. The Relationship Profiling process captures information about the detailed operation of relationship interactions from the point of view of both participating entities. It comprises up to three steps:

- detailed analysis of the Relationship Profiles of a Relationship Interaction
- specifying the ideal profile of a Relationship Interaction
- alternative Relationship Profiling

Detailed Analysis of the Relationship Profiles of a Relationship Interaction

This step captures detailed information about a relationship interaction. This information is structured in terms of the relationship dimensions and elements identified in the previous chapters. It provides information about the "softer" elements of relationships, such as emotion, control, and structure, as well as the "harder" operational details. When looking at the details of relationships it is necessary to decide which dimensions and elements to include in the detailed analysis. In the example used below all of the dimensions and elements will be used except the bonding element. This is because it would be difficult to phrase questions about bonding for the subject matter under investigation. If, however, during the analysis it became clear that bonding was in fact an important element, a way would have to be found to include it.

Relationship Profiling provides a central core for controlled Relationship Analysis and relationship development. The profile identifies the level of operation of each relationship element from a number of different perspectives. The operation of a relationship can be viewed in four ways:

TABLE 6.3
The Relationship Dimensions and Elements Used in the Car Dealership Example

Relationship Dimension	Relationship Element
Control	Accountability
	Authority
	Dexterity
	Responsibility
Emotion	Approval
	Fairness
	Respect
	Satisfaction
	Trust
Operation	Accuracy of information
	Availability of resources
	Capability
	Ease of operation
	Knowledge
	Responsiveness
Structure	Flexibility
	Formality
	Openness

- the Relationship Interaction performance of an entity as seen by that entity; this is known as the "actual performance"
- the Relationship Interaction performance of an entity as expected by that entity; this is known as the "expected performance"
- the Relationship Interaction performance for that entity as seen by the other entity; this is known as the "other actual performance"
- the Relationship Interaction performance for that entity as expected by the other entity; this is known as the "other expected performance"

The performance level is identified by allocating a score from 1 to 5 for each element of the relationship (in the same manner as for the Relationship Alignment Table). This indicates the level of performance for an entity in managing that relationship element. The different profiles can then be compared to develop an understanding of the relationship interaction.

The relationship profile scores are usually gathered by questionnaire. Table 6.4 shows a sample Relationship Profile Table with each of the four views of the relationship plus the ideal profile and alternative supplier performance scores, which will be discussed latter. The scores enable a relationship to be analyzed from the point of view of both entities or entity types involved.

Specifying the Ideal Profile of a Relationship Interaction

An ideal Relationship Profile can be created to show how a relationship should be operating. This ideal profile is created by defining how you wish a relationship to operate and

TABLE 6.4
A Relationship Profile Table

Dimension	Element	Actual	Other Actual	Expected	Other Expected	Ideal Profile	Alternative
Control	Authority						
	Accountability						
	Dexterity						
	Responsibility						
Emotion	Approval						
	Fairness of exchange						
	Respect						
	Satisfaction						
	Trust						
Operation	Accuracy of information						
	Availability of resources						
	Capability						
	Ease of operation						
	Knowledge						
	Responsiveness						
Structure	Flexibility						
	Formality						
	Openness						

calculating the ideal performance scores for each relationship element. Ideal profiling provides a statement of the strategic expectations of relationship performance and is particularly informative when attempting to engineer change in an organization. This is particularly valuable when investigating the two situationally specific dimensions of control and structure. The elements in these two dimensions do not have absolute values, so a higher score is not necessarily a better score. This therefore requires that the appropriate level of each element be identified for each entity in each relationship in question.

For example, an organization may be reducing its management and control structures and creating a new position of managing consultant, rather than the previous controlling administrative manager. The relationship between that new managing consultant and the other consultants in the group may well be different from that between the consultants and the old administrative manager. In particular, the consultants may take on greater levels of responsibility and accountability, with the managing consultant taking on a guiding rather than a decision-making role. As a result the balance of responsibility and accountability that the respective consultants and the managing consultant have, in the relationships they form around the processes they operate, will be relatively balanced. The impact of that change on the consultants involved can then be identified, action taken to address the effects of that change, and monitoring put in place to review the success of the change.

Alternative Relationship Profiling

An alternative relationship profile can be created to identify how well a relationship is being operated in relation to other alternatives in the marketplace or within the organization. The exact nature of the information captured about alternatives will depend on the issue being analyzed and the nature of the market. For example, to gather a complete view of the Relationship Profile of a market, alternative profiles could be collected for the best, average, and worst performers in that market. These alternative profiles provide key strategic information about the "softer" elements of market and internal relationships to support effective strategic decision making.

Analysis of the Relationship Profiles

The ability to identify and compare actual, expected, other, ideal, and alternative Relationship Profiles provides a powerful capability for evaluating and managing relationships. It can be used to

- identify entity relationship performance and any misalignment
- identify the impact of changes to markets, organizations, and individuals and evaluate the necessary adjustments in the way that relationships are operated to respond to those changes
- view the change over time in the relationship profile of markets, organizations, groups, and individuals

The profiling process also raises many issues that often would not otherwise be considered. Traditional analysis of the relationship between an organization and its customers would not usually consider all of the elements identified in Relationship Dynamics.

This part of the analysis process depends on the ability to interpret the information effectively and to generate effective responses. It identifies the detailed nature of operation of the relationship interaction; then, if needed, it indicates effective strategies or action to address any issues of concern. The information that is collected provides the basis for sophisticated analysis. It provides the capability to compare the interactions between the different relationship views, e.g.,

- relationship performance as seen by both entities
- relationship performance as seen by one entity compared to the performance that entity expects

- relationship performance as seen by one entity compared to the performance that the other entity expects of that entity
- all of the other views of the relationship compared to the desired ideal relationship performance
- performance of an entity compared to the best, or next best, alternative

This information enables the relationship to be analyzed in terms of actual performance, expected performance, and the points of view of both participants. Table 6.5 shows the scores generated for the car-dealership–retail-customer servicing-and-repairs relationship interaction for the performance of the car dealership. The performance scores show

- the dealership's view of its own performance in the relationship
- the retail customer's view of the dealership's performance in the relationship
- the dealership's expectation of its own performance in the relationship
- the retail customer's expectation of the dealership's performance in the relationship
- the dealership's strategic goal for their performance in the relationship
- the customer's view of the performance of the best alternative to the dealership being analyzed

The information in the Profiling Analysis Table can be viewed in many ways. Three of these possible views are shown below. This view of the relationship, shown in Table 6.6A, identifies that the customer's perception of the dealership's performance was lower than the dealership's view of

TABLE 6.5
Completed Relationship Profiling Table

Analysis Issue: Falling sales of top line models
Relationship Interaction: Servicing & repairs
Main Entity: Luxury car dealership
Other Entity: Retail customer

Dimension	Element	Dealership's View of Its Own Performance	Customer's View of the Dealership's Performance	Dealership's Expectation of Its Own Performance	Customer's Expectation of the Dealership's Performance	Dealership's Ideal Profile	Customer's View of the Best Alternative Supplier
Control	Authority	3	3	4	3	3	3
	Accountability	4	2	5	5	5	4
	Dexterity	4	3	5	5	5	4
	Responsibility	4	3	5	5	5	4
Emotion	Approval	3	3	4	5	5	4
	Fairness of exchange	4	3	5	5	5	4
	Respect	4	3	5	5	5	4
	Satisfaction	3	3	5	5	5	4
	Trust	4	3	5	5	5	4
Operation	Accuracy of information	3	3	4	5	5	4
	Availability of resources	3	3	5	5	5	4
	Capability	4	3	5	5	5	5
	Ease of operation	4	3	5	5	5	5
	Knowledge	4	3	5	5	5	5
	Responsiveness	3	3	5	5	5	5
Structure	Flexibility	3	3	4	4	5	3
	Formality	3	3	3	3	3	4
	Openness	3	3	4	4	5	3

TABLE 6.6A

The Customer's View vs. the Dealership's View of the Dealership's Performance in the Relationship

Dimension	Element	Customer's View of the Dealership's Performance	Dealership's View of Its Own Performance	Difference
Control	Authority	3	3	0
	Accountability	2	4	-2
	Dexterity	3	4	-1
	Responsibility	3	4	-1
Emotion	Approval	3	3	0
	Fairness of exchange	3	4	-1
	Respect	3	4	-1
	Satisfaction	3	3	0
	Trust	3	4	-1
Operation	Accuracy of information	3	3	0
	Availability of resources	3	3	0
	Capability	3	4	-1
	Ease of operation	3	4	-1
	Knowledge	3	4	-1
	Responsiveness	3	3	0
Structure	Flexibility	3	3	0
	Formality	3	3	0
	Openness	3	3	0
		2.94	3.5	-0.56

itself. This difference is found in the control, emotion, and operation dimensions. The nature of the data and the underlying dimensions is such that you cannot take the specific numeric values and calculate specific conclusions. Rather, you can take a general indication of issues and their type. Far from being a limitation, the use of general indicators is extremely powerful in this context.

It enables us to investigate phenomena that have previously been difficult to identify in a meaningful, mutually understood fashion, such as "perceived quality." In the example above three different aspects of the relationship have been identified as problematic. These aspects of control, emotion, and operation are likely to be interlinked, in that

TABLE 6.6B

The Dealership's View of the Dealership's Performance in the
Relationship vs. the Dealership's Ideal View

Dimension	Element	Dealership's View of Its Own Performance	Dealership's Ideal Profile	Difference
Control	Authority	3	3	0
	Accountability	4	5	-1
	Dexterity	4	5	-1
	Responsibility	4	5	-1
Emotion	Approval	3	5	-2
	Fairness of exchange	4	5	-1
	Respect	4	5	-1
	Satisfaction	3	5	-2
	Trust	4	5	-1
Operation	Accuracy of information	3	5	-2
	Availability of resources	3	5	-2
	Capability	4	5	-1
	Ease of operation	4	5	-1
	Knowledge	4	5	-1
	Responsiveness	3	5	-2
Structure	Flexibility	3	5	-2
	Formality	3	3	0
	Openness	3	5	-2
		3.5	4.78	-1.28

an improvement in the dealership's operational capability to service and repair the cars, combined with an increase in their accountability, will probably improve the customer's emotional perception of the relationship. Before we look at the implications of the information further, we will evaluate the other two views.

This second view, shown in Table 6.6B, identifies that the dealership is not performing to its desired strategic goal. (In fact, a comparison with the full Table 6.5 will show that the dealership is also performing less well than it expected to in the specific situation.) This raises some serious questions for the dealership, which is not responding to the needs of the market as it believes it should be. This information, to-

TABLE 6.7

The Customer's View of the Dealership's Performance in the Relationship Compared to the Customer's View of the Best Alternative Supplier

Dimension	Element	Customer's View of the Dealership's Performance	Customer's View of the Best Alternative Supplier	Difference
Control	Authority	3	3	0
	Accountability	2	4	-2
	Dexterity	3	4	-1
	Responsibility	3	4	-1
Emotion	Approval	3	4	-1
	Fairness of exchange	3	4	-1
	Respect	3	4	-1
	Satisfaction	3	4	-1
	Trust	3	4	-1
Operation	Accuracy of information	3	4	-1
	Availability of resources	3	4	-1
	Capability	3	4	-1
	Ease of operation	3	5	-2
	Knowledge	3	5	-2
	Responsiveness	3	5	-2
Structure	Flexibility	3	3	0
	Formality	3	4	-1
	Openness	3	3	0
		2.94	4	-1.06

gether with the next view, will provide a powerful set of information from which the dealership can start to consider and address the situation.

This third view, shown in Table 6.7, demonstrates that the customer base also deals with other suppliers who perform significantly better than the dealership being analyzed. Taking all three views into consideration, the car dealership is meeting neither its own expectations nor those of the customer, and is performing worse than other suppliers in the marketplace. The car dealership is not providing the high level of servicing and repair performance expected to justify the premium pricing of both the car and the subsequent servicing and repairs. It is important to note that we have not just identified that the retail customer is dissatisfied with the operational aspects of servicing and repairs. We have also identified that

- the accountability and responsibility the car dealership takes is too low
- both the operational and control dimension issues have impacted on the emotional acceptance of the retail customer of the whole luxury-car experience with this dealer
- the competition performs near perfectly in the operation dimension, but there is a potential gap to be exploited in the structure, emotion, and control dimensions

It may be, however, that the resource cost involved in resolving the problems compromises the viability of the dealership. At the higher level of analysis, the dealership scored itself a 2 for viability in terms of the current operation of the relationship. It obviously needs to take action to address the problems in this relationship. The dealership must balance the need for action in each relationship dimension with the requirement for viable operation. It needs to decide whether it wishes to address its poor performance or to change its product to one that is in line with the Relationship Profile that it desires with its customers. It may decide to give up the luxury-car franchise and supply another make of car that does not require such a high overall relationship performance. Alternatively, it may adjust the manner in which it responds to customer issues and requests so as to improve their perception of its accountability and responsibility, and also respond to the higher operational performance of its competitors. In doing this it could identify ways of responding to customer issues and requests that deliver exceptional response, so as to attempt to improve its customer relationships and capture more of the market from alternative suppliers. Whatever its decision, it needs to respond to the wider elements of the relationship, not just the ability of its mechanics to service and repair cars.

Many business problems will be found, on analysis, to involve the four dimensions of control, emotion, operation, and structure, rather than merely a basic operational dimension. The lack of previously available tools to assist people in dealing with the wider four-dimensional relationship issues has often led to difficulties in problem identification and resolution. Relationship Analysis enables fast and effective analysis of situations, so that the nature of a problem can be identified. In many cases where the problem is control-, emotion-, or structure-based and any operational issues are relatively simple, Relationship Analysis provides a direct statement of the problem and identifies a possible solution. Where the problem is in a detailed person, resource, process, or information issue, Relationship Analysis provides an effective technique to identify the main problem and the other contributing elements that will need to be addressed.

In summary, Relationship Analysis provides three steps that develop an understanding of the operation of any relationship:

• Relationship Scoping,
• Relationship Alignment, and
• Relationship Profiling.

Relationship Scoping and Relationship Alignment are very effective as a starting point for strategic and speculative analysis. This initial focus on relationships provides a framework upon which to identify relationship and other issues. Most problems occurring within organizations will have an impact on the relationships in the organization. Thus an initial focus on relationships leads to a more comprehensive range of issues being identified.

Relationship Profiling provides a detailed analysis of specific relationships interactions. It should be applied to specific situations that need to be understood, developed, or optimized. It provides a similar level of detail about the operation of relationships that existing methods for detailed process and information analysis do in their dimensions. Therefore, when changes are being considered or applied to organizations, Relationship Profiling should be used as part of the complete toolkit to understand and subsequently manage such change. Any change that does not include an understanding of relationship issues, will usually encounter problems.

The Relationship Scoping, Alignment, and Profiling analysis processes integrate with each other, providing a consistent approach that analyzes all levels of relationships and their impact. They provide a systematic process for the internal and external analysis of organizations. These techniques enable organizations and individuals to evaluate the situations they encounter in an efficient and effective manner. The focus on relationships enables the analysis process to capture issues of many types, which can then be analyzed in more detail with other specific analytical techniques such as process or information analysis, if required.

CHAPTER 7

EVALUATING
RELATIONSHIPS

Relationships are influenced by the perceptions of each entity in a relationship and wider considerations that arise from the operation of individuals and groups in society. In this chapter the relationship is evaluated in terms of this wider social and economic environment though the introduction of two new categories, Relationship Styles and Relationship Influences.

Relationships can be driven primarily by one of the relationship dimensions or by a combination of them. The relationship profile reflects the contribution of each of the four relationship dimensions, from the point of view of each entity. This mix of contributions can be either balanced across the relationship dimensions or weighted in favor of specific dimensions. The balance of that influence has a major impact on the operation of a relationship.

An *emotion-driven relationship* is a manifestation of an overwhelming desire for emotional satisfaction, to the exclusion of the other dimensions. Such a relationship aims to

Figure 7.1

The influences upon relationships

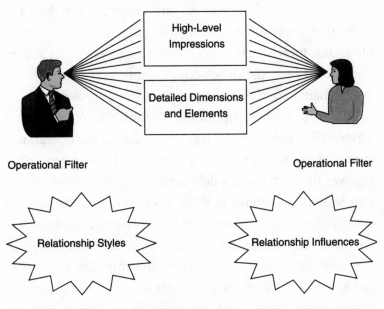

satisfy the emotion dimension directly; this may result in behavior that denies effective performance in the other dimensions. Such relationships may, therefore, lack the rigor of a defined and objective goal and an identifiable control mechanism. For example, when two people first fall in love they often focus on satisfying the emotion dimension of their relationship, to the exclusion of almost everything else. The focus on the emotion dimension is sometimes so great that the two people behave in a seemingly irrational manner that appears to compromise other aspects of their lives. But equally, emotion-driven relationships can overcome what seem to others impossible practical obstacles.

An *operation-driven relationship* focuses on the achievement of definable goals. All relationships can be judged on the operation dimension. Claims that a relationship should be solely judged on the other dimensions are usually attempts to evade the issue of performance. This does not mean that a relationship cannot be judged on the other dimensions, merely that it should usually generate an effective operational outcome to be seen as wholly effective.

The main aim of one of the entities in a *control-driven relationship* is to take control of the relationship. While control is normally dependent on the satisfaction of the operational and/or emotional dimensions, a control-driven relationship involves the creation of a deliberate imbalance in the control profile of the relationship. With this type of relationship, the activity that is performed to generate effective outcomes in the other dimensions is secondary to the desire to take control from the other party in the relationship. Once this control is established, the requirement for effective satisfaction of the other dimensions lessens. Control-driven relationships will tend to have defined structures; in general, they will range from somewhat formal and closed to highly formal and closed. As the control dimension is driving the relationship, a structure must be adopted to demonstrate when action, related to the emotion and operation dimension, should be curtailed to remain in line with the control requirements. This will happen even if, in a purely objective view, the curtailed action appears to be the best.

Within control-driven relationships there is a sanction that can be used, that cuts across all other considerations—physical force. Physical force is often applied when the social and psychological dynamic of relationships breaks down. It provides the ultimate control mechanism. Physical force enables a specific outcome to be forced onto a relationship. A relationship cannot, however, be maintained over time through force alone. Relationships require the participation of both parties. If one party refuses to take part in the relationship, physical force cannot guarantee that participation. Long-term relationships must address the social and psychological dynamic or remain in an escalating cycle of conflict until the relationship is destroyed. Physical force is therefore only really effective as a short-term mechanism. Over the longer term, physical force will deny the real goals of the relationship and become an end in itself.

Relationships are rarely driven by the *structure dimension*. This is only likely to occur when the reason for the relationship has disappeared and the structure of operation is all that remains of the relationship. The structure dimension is rarely manipulated as an end in itself. For example, the desire of one entity to control the other results in a primary focus on the elements in the control dimension. Elements of the structure dimension will then be used to support the required levels of control.

These relationship drivers have a primary effect on the operation of relationships.

INFLUENCES ON RELATIONSHIPS

Relationships operate within a dynamic social environment, which itself impacts back on the relationship. To understand the operation of relationships within this dynamic environment requires that the various influences can be identified and accounted for. Three different types of influences have a major impact on relationships:

- group roles
- dynamic transaction roles
- personal interaction levels

The different roles and transaction levels identified in Figure 7.2 have not been chosen for their theoretical purity. Rather, they have been chosen because they provide powerful indicators about the operation of relationships in practice. The different elements identified are not mutually exclusive. A person can perform many group and dynamic transactional roles, at a number of personal interaction levels, and within combined relationship styles. This overlap of elements often makes it difficult to understand and improve the operation of a relationship. Relationship Dynamics provides a structure for teasing out each element and identifying its contribution to the relationship within the context of the goals and scope of the relationship between the specific people involved.

In the social environment we use the concept of stereotypes and roles to classify behavior so that we can build up an understanding of a person's likely behavior in characteristic situations.

> A stereotype is the norm and expectations associated with a person. The behavioural expectations associated with stereotypes are usually general and somewhat vague. A role is the norm and expectations associated with a person in a social structure and its interactions with other roles in that social structure. The behavioural expectations associated with roles are usually specific. This specificity puts constraints on behaviour and makes behaviour in a role within a relationship predictable.
>
> Peter Kelvin, *The Bases of Social Behaviour* (1973)

In many situations we act both as an individual and as a member of a group. Further, we perform one or more roles. A role is the expectation of how a person will perform in the dynamic interaction of a relationship. This expectation provides information about how a person will behave, and will usually implicitly affect the manner in which a relationship

Figure 7.2
Relationship characteristics

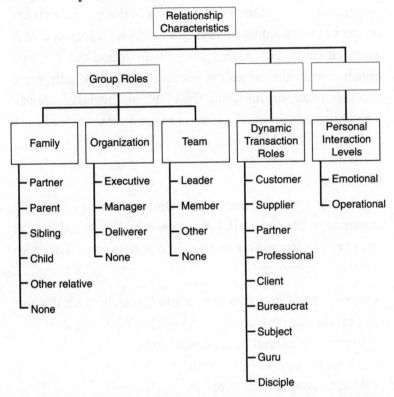

operates. Relationship Dynamics is not initially concerned with how the entity in question came to be performing that role; rather, it is initially concerned with the manner in which that role is being performed. In subsequent analysis of issues arising from this performance, we may wish to understand all of the issues surrounding that entity in that role and how the issues can be best addressed.

GROUP ROLES

There are many groups that we belong to over our lifetime. These groups can usefully be categorized into three basic types: families, organizations, and teams. A person can be placed into one, two, or all of these groups when they operate relationships. Membership of each of the groups impacts on the nature of a relationship. For example, a person who is an executive in an organization is likely to find that his relationship with his immediate subordinate will be different if that subordinate is his father than it would be if the subordinate is not a relative. The roles conferred by membership of these groups affect the operation of a relationship.

Families

A family is a social group united through bonds of kinship or marriage. These bonds have a powerful emotional tie that can override immediate practical considerations. The roles in a family group are:

- *partner:* to tie together two families, usually with the aim of producing children
- *parent:* to bear and nurture children
- *sibling:* to support other siblings
- *child:* to grow and develop
- *other:* looser ties, which include responsibility for other family members

The family group roles center around the notion of responsibility for other family members. The closer the relationship between family members is to the parent-child relationship, the greater the responsibility that is both expected and usually taken.

Organizations

An organization is a formally arranged group of people who subscribe to a common overall goal. It is likely to be too large for each member to form well-defined personal relationships with all of the other members. Organizations come in many forms such as commercial, military, and voluntary. The size of an organization requires that it has a formal command and control structure to enable its effective operation. The roles in an organization are:

- *executive*: to make effective decisions in changing situations
- *manager*: to enable those being managed to implement policies and procedures in line with the aims of the organization
- *deliverer*: to carry out defined tasks
- *other*: looser ties which include responsibility for organization outcomes and members.

Organizations have to focus on this structural element in order to perform effectively. But when this structural focus becomes too great, an organization can forget its primary aims and put too much energy into maintaining the structure for its own sake.

Teams

A team is a "small number of people with complementary skills who are committed to a common purpose, performance goals, and approach for which they hold themselves accountable" (Katzenbach & Smith, 1993). The small size of a team enables each member of the team to generate a personal relationship with the other team members. The roles in a team are these:

- *leader*: to provide direction and purpose for the team
- *member*: to support the other team members and act appropriately

- *other*: hybrid roles combining leadership and membership can occur

The small size and shared focus of teams make them powerful instruments of operation. Their generation of strong personal relationships often causes a team to generate its own goals, which may or may not be in line with the goals of the larger organization to which the team belongs. There are many examples of this happening—particularly with new-product development in large organizations. New computer systems, trains, and even steel plants have been developed by "renegade" teams in organizations.

DYNAMIC TRANSACTION ROLES

Each time people interact with one another they are creating a dynamic transaction that is unique in terms of the participants, their roles, and the time and context of the interaction. Every relationship interaction has an element of general exchange that underlies the specific exchange being undertaken. In support of this general exchange the participants take on the roles of supplier and customer. In some cases the interaction is more complicated than a general exchange. In such cases those involved in the relationship interaction are entering it performing other roles that make their position in the relationship more specific. These roles, such as a partner or a professional, may also define the role of the other participant. The dynamic transaction roles are:

General Exchange
- *customer*: to receive goods or services
- *supplier*: to supply goods or services

Specific Roles

- *partner:* to share resources and responsibility with the other person, team, group, or organization in the relationship in order to achieve a shared goal
- *professional:* to provide a high level of performance and/or service in specific tasks
- *client:* to provide effective information to enable a professional to carry out their task effectively
- *bureaucrat:* to carry out organizational policies and procedures
- *subject:* to be subject to the policies and procedures of the organization
- *guru:* to provide emotional and/or intellectual leadership
- *disciple:* to follow the emotional and/or intellectual leadership of a guru

For each of the specific roles distinctive performance characteristics can be defined. These performance characteristics make it possible to identify both how a person *is* operating a relationship and how a person *should* operate a relationship if he wishes to perform one of these roles. Table 7.1 shows these distinctive performance characteristics.

The table shows four scores, which mean the following:

- H: A person performing that dynamic transaction role performs above average on all of the elements within the identified relationship dimensions or specific elements.
- M: A person performing that dynamic transaction role performs average on all of the elements within the identified relationship dimensions or specific elements.
- L: A person performing that dynamic transaction role performs worse than average on all of the elements within

TABLE 7.1
Distinctive Performance Characteristics of Dynamic Transaction Roles

	Partner	Professional	Client	Bureaucrat	Subject	Guru	Disciple
Control	M/H	H	L	H	L	H	L
Emotion	M/H	L/M	M/H	L	H	H	H
Operation	—	H	—	—	—	—	—
Flexibility	—	—	—	L	—	L/M	L/M
Formality	—	—	—	H	H	H	H
Openness	H	—	H	L	—	L/M	L/M

the identified relationship dimensions or specific elements.

• —: There is no characteristic score for this dynamic transaction role relationship dimension or specific element combination.

These values identify the expected performance of each of the dynamic transaction roles. This characteristic performance can be used to discover if the roles are being performed correctly and the implications for the performance of any of the roles.

PERSONAL INTERACTION LEVEL

Each relationship is operated at a specific level of intensity. Two different levels have been identified:

• *emotional:* a transaction that involves people in emotionally focused behavior that is independent of specific operational outcomes
• *operational:* a transaction that focuses on the generation of a specific operational outcome

These different levels can affect the operation of the relationship very powerfully. The interference effect of the personal interaction level can often override all of the other aspects of a relationship.

RELATIONSHIP STYLES

The dynamic transaction roles are often performed in pairs. Indeed, many of these roles can only be performed if the other party to the relationship performs the required opposing role. We have identified five often-encountered pairs of dynamic transaction roles. These we have termed "Relationship Styles." Relationship Styles are direct and powerful. They provide us with additional information and understanding about relationships because they show how a relationship operates from both sides. This enables us to quickly understand the operation of our relationships and whether or not they are appropriate for the desired outcomes. The five styles are:

- market style
- partnership style
- bureaucratic style
- professional style
- charismatic style

Not all relationships correspond to these five styles, but relationship styles do provide a very useful base from which to gain a fast appreciation of the operation of any relationship. They can also be easily validated against objective observable behaviors. Relationship Styles provide a mechanism that produces fast understanding of complex situations and makes clear the nature of the interaction between entities. They achieve this because they do not attempt to tie every deterministic element down, but rather accept the ever changing and dynamic reality of relationships. While developing the concept of Relationship Styles we also encountered Max Boisot's concept of Transactional Strategies (see Max Boisot, *Information and Organizations,* 1987). Transactional Strategies are similar to Relationship Styles but do not spring from the same basic analysis of relationships. The focus in Transactional Strategies is primarily on the nature of the information passed in the transactions, and the resulting groupings of transaction types is somewhat different. This concept of the nature of the information being passed in transactions provides an additional element to Relationship Styles and has been incorporated in the resulting concept of a Relationship Style.

The Market-Style Relationship

Market styles of relationships involve one entity performing the dynamic transaction role of a supplier and the other the dynamic transaction role of a customer. They are based on a relationship that is only operating in order to satisfy a general exchange. Market-style relationships are universal and occur in all areas of life. They do not just occur when a product or service is being purchased; they occur when any exchange is made between two entities. A pure market-style relationship will have the following attributes:

- a focus on the specific product or service to be exchanged
- a relatively impersonal input from both entities
- widely available information that promotes the choice of alternatives, if available
- no requirement for the seller and purchaser to share beliefs and values
- a formal or informal basis for operation as required
- goals that are agreed by negotiation

The exact profile of a market-style relationship is determined by the conditions that relate to each specific interaction. These are determined by the relative capability and situation of the supplier and customer. For example, where a relationship is established to purchase goods that are in short supply or oversupply, the key driver in that relationship will be the control dimension. This situation occurs when there is monopolistic or oligopolistic manipulation of a market. When there is a balance between supply and demand, as in the "classic" market situation, the other dimensions come into play more strongly. The purchaser may then focus on:

- the specific capabilities of the product or service (the operation dimension)
- the emotional outcome generated by the transaction (the emotion dimension)
- the manner in which the product or service is provided (the structure dimension)

From this it can be seen that, where there is a market-style relationship and the market is not being affected by supplier manipulation or resource limitation, the other relationship dimensions can come into play more strongly.

The Partnership-Style Relationship

Partnership-style relationships involve both entities performing the dynamic transaction role of a partner. These relationships focus on effective operation between two entities operating much like one aggregate entity. Their basic interaction is therefore based on shared goals and openness. The exact nature of the role depends on the nature of the partnership. The partnership-style relationship will have the following attributes:

Figure 7.3

The partnership relationship style

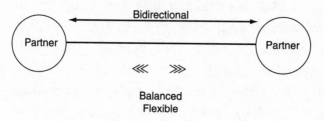

Relationship Weights may vary, but an effective partnership will always adjust.

Requires agreed-upon Goal, Roles, and Scope

- a focus on the specific product or service to be exchanged or shared
- a personal input from both entities
- operates on the basis of shared information
- both partners need to share beliefs and values
- a formal or informal basis, as required
- goals agreed upon by negotiation

This profile is determined by the conditions that relate to each specific interaction but will, at a minimum, involve the sharing of information or control. The sharing of information and control is what differentiates a partnership from a market-style relationship. A partnership will usually also involve a sharing of beliefs and values and some form of personal input from the participating entities. The difference between a partnership and a market relationship explains why it is often extremely difficult to change a relationship from a market-based one to a partnership-based one. Such a change requires that the whole basis for the interaction be changed from separate goals and behavior to shared goals and behavior.

For example, many banks are trying to develop partner-ship-style relationships with their business customers. How-ever, a bank is seen by its business customers as participat-ing with them in a market-style relationship, in which it performs the role of a supplier of funds—on its own terms. It is difficult for the bank to change the shared relationship style to one of partnership, because the dynamic transaction role of partner requires a profile of relationship different from the dynamic transaction role of a simple supplier of funds. Partnership-style relationships require:

• a wider set of operational interactions
• a greater emotional commitment
• a change in the nature of the control so that it is shared

Many banks have introduced leaflets, brochures, and seminar series in order to stimulate this change in role. The only change in operation they have made, however, has been to set up a few meetings with clients and to offer more prod-ucts in an attempt to add value. This adding of value is only affecting the operational dimension. Partnership is a differ-ent style of relationship from market style. It requires a change in the nature of all four dimensions to turn a market-style relationship into a partnership-style relationship. None of those banks are making serious attempts to change the nature of their relationships. As a result, they are finding it hard to develop any meaningful partnerships with their cus-tomer base. They are picking up some business based on the new services available, but they have not developed real partnership.

Those banks have not really understood what partnership means and are playing with the term. They see "partner-ship" as increasing their own business turnover and profitability, while maintaining the same levels of control as before over those they lend money to. They are using partnership as a marketing concept to generate discussion with their customers rather than changing their own role in the relationship. If they believe that real partnerships would bring improved returns, they are missing an opportunity to build such partnerships. If they are just looking to mount marketing campaigns to attract attention at a time of economic recovery, they may be succeeding in their aims. The problem with this last approach is that they are alienating many customers and employees who believe that a true partnership-style relationship would benefit both the banks and their customers.

The Bureaucratic-Style Relationship

This relationship style involves one entity performing the dynamic transaction role of bureaucrat and the other the dynamic transaction role of subject. Bureaucracies are focused on the structure and control dimensions. As such they tend to create relatively inflexible and formal modes of operation. The bureaucratic-style relationship will have the following attributes:

- It is impersonal, with no requirement for shared values.
- The bureaucracy has a dominant position, provided it operates both appropriately and within its sphere of influence.
- It tends to operate in a fragmented, hierarchical manner.
- The initial requirement for the relationship is usually well defined. However, the operation of the relationship is often esoteric and deliberately hidden by the bureaucracy, which can sometimes modify the relationship against the intention of the initial requirement.

Figure 7.4

The bureaucratic-style relationship

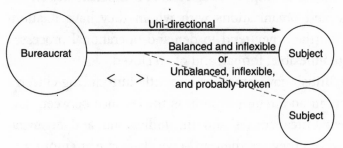

Relationship Weights vary—the bureaucrat has the control as long as that control is backed by legislation or position.

Does not require agreed-upon Goal, Roles, and Scope

• When the goals of each entity are in conflict, legal challenges usually result.

Bureaucratic forms of operation have developed to provide for the administration of large organizations. Such organizations may be governmental, commercial, or voluntary. Characteristic of this form of operation is the generation of internal relationships to support a higher organizational purpose. Relationships within bureaucratic organizations are created to enable information and decisions to flow in a hierarchical manner. The hierarchical structure distributes interaction with external entities broadly among many people inside the hierarchical organization. The internal structure of bureaucratic organizations has a major impact on their relationships with others. It generates a hidden process, of which only a part is seen by outsiders. Even within the bureaucracy, it is often the case that few of the people understand the full process.

Bureaucracies tend to define the ground rules that others who wish, or are required, to have a relationship with them must operate. Bureaucracies assume a position of authority and knowledge, but often fail to accept the appropriate level of responsibility and accountability that goes with that position. They often impose a high level of responsibility on the people and organizations with whom they have relationships. Further, they tend to demand operational processes that are inflexible, formal, and often closed.

The British government is currently introducing citizen's charters in an attempt to redress the balance between government bureaucracies and the individuals and organizations whom they are there to serve. They are attempting to improve the operation of government institutions by increasing their operational capability, in terms of ease of use and responsiveness. From this they wish to improve the emotional dimension of the relationship, resulting (it is hoped) in more people feeling respect and approval for the government organizations.

The major difficulty is that the basic characteristics of bureaucracies are much more difficult to change. By their nature, government organizations operate on the basis of statutes and government directives. This is a slow process that usually requires time to turn general principles into effective operation. In Britain many of these directives are based on Acts of Parliament that are poorly drafted and have been produced, seemingly, with little concern for how they will have to be implemented in real life. The Child Support Agency and Community Charge legislation are examples of these.

Bureaucratic institutions tend to focus on the processes and procedures of their operation rather than on its goals and scope. Often, they lose sight of the outcomes they are there to generate. This is caused by the very process that they use to manage their sheer size and complexity: a hierarchical structure and fragmented decision making. More than this, the legal requirements on government bureaucracies are such that in many cases they have a general duty to operate for the good of the people in the country. However, this has not been interpreted by the courts as providing the same duty at a more meaningful level, toward the individual. As a result of this generalized legal underpinning, government bureaucracy has a high level of authority but does not have full responsibility for taking action, nor full accountability for the results of its action.

That contrasts with organizations operating in the commercial environment. There the discipline of the market always reacts to poor performance by reducing the business's profits. There is no fundamental mechanism that operates on government bureaucracies in the same manner. This lack of a mechanism to force the discipline of responsibility and accountability on government bureaucracies, together with the problems of bureaucratic organization, means that the citizen's charter is unlikely to succeed. What is needed to improve operation significantly is a mechanism to generate proper accountability. Without this mechanism the citizen's charter will result in limited operational improvement but no fundamental change.

Commercially based organizations may also have bureaucratic-style relationships. As identified above, such organizations have to adjust the nature of their relationships when the discipline of the market forces such a change. This can be seen in the relative decline of the "giant" organizations of the 1960s, 1970s, and 1980s. Where markets have become more competitive, as in the computer industry, the overheads imposed by bureaucratic-style relationships, which restricted speed and effectiveness of action, have been removed. This has enabled the smaller, more dynamic, operationally focused organizations to prosper at the expense of the older, more bureaucratic organizations. In the information technology sector, companies such as IBM have not been able to change the style of their internal and external relationships fast enough. Their hierarchical, bureaucratic legacy has reduced their competitiveness. Other companies such as Hewlett-Packard, Compaq, Intel, and Microsoft have managed to focus on market- and partnership-style relationships. This more direct focus on the outcome of their relationships, rather than on the bureaucratic structure of their relationships, enables them to respond more directly to both their customers and their partners. The command-and-control structures of the bureaucratic style of relationship seem to produce less effective responses than the more directly focused market- and partnership-style relationships in today's fast-changing social and economic environment.

The Professional-Style Relationship

Professional-style relationships involve one entity performing the dynamic transaction role of a professional and the other entity the dynamic transaction role of a client. The professional provides a service to the client that the client needs, in the form of a specialist services. The professional-style relationship will have the following attributes:

- a focus on the specific product or service to be provided
- involvement on a personal or impersonal basis, dependent upon the specific operational requirements
- operation on the basis of shared client information—but usually esoteric professional information

- no requirement that the professional and the client share beliefs and values
- usually, operation on a formal basis, as required
- goals agreed upon through negotiation—but the lack of knowledge held by the client may affect that negotiation

The status of a professional in society is dependent on a professional's ability to deliver effective operational results. The emotional acceptance of a professional by a client is only justified by the professional's ability to perform effectively. Because professionals tend to have a skill that is not fully distributed in the population, they have a relatively high level of control over those nonprofessionals who wish to develop a relationship with them.

For example, the legal and medical professions are well known for treating their clients in a dismissive fashion. Many doctors and lawyers feel that their clients cannot understand the detail that they are dealing with. As a result, they often do not attempt to share that knowledge and decision making with the client. This tendency has lessened in recent years, but is still widespread.

Figure 7.5
The professional-style relationship

Relationship Weights vary—the professional has the control as long as that control is backed by his capability of operation.

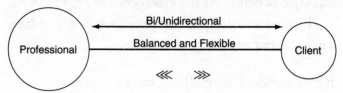

Requires agreed Goal, Roles, and Scope

Professional relationships are dependent on the exact nature of the professional's skill. This is often made out to be highly esoteric in nature, with a bar on knowledge for the uninitiated. Professionals have tended to form associations to protect their body of knowledge. Other professionals who share that body of knowledge can then develop partnership-style relationships with each other. This creates a more effective barrier between those who have membership of the professional body and those who do not. This high level of ownership of knowledge and control is balanced by the requirement for a professional to perform effectively.

If a professional consistently fails to perform in the manner expected then he will be unable to fulfill his role as a professional and will lose the emotional acceptance of the client and the support of his fellow professionals. That balancing mechanism of a focus on the effectiveness of outcomes creates a different situation to the bureaucratic and charismatic styles, which have no similar balancing mechanism.

The Charismatic-Style Relationship

Charismatic-style relationships involve one entity performing the dynamic transaction role of guru and the other entity performing the dynamic transaction role of disciple. This relationship style depends on the emergence of "faith" in the disciple. The charismatic-style relationship is likely to have the following characteristics:

- It is highly personal, with shared values.
- The guru has a dominant role.

- The disciples are submissive to the values and goals of the guru.
- The nature of the relationship is often esoteric to the uninitiated.
- The relationship is likely to be relatively closed and formal.
- Goals are defined by the guru.

An example of this type of relationship is that between charismatic religious leaders and their followers. The charismatic-style relationship is characterized by a high degree of emotional investment by the followers, with the guru having a high perceived level of control. This imbalance of the emotion and control dimensions occurs when a blind faith is generated in a leader or companion. This can lead to a willingness to believe the leader or companion in situations when they contradict observed reality.

Gurus require a massive emotional investment on the part of their disciples. This emotional investment is required to generate the control that the guru has over the disciple. In giving up control the disciple is accepting that he is subject to the wishes of the guru. Note that the guru does not necessarily have a high focus on the operation dimension. Gurus tend to ignore the operational dimension and claim positive emotional outcomes instead.

This relationship style is most powerfully seen in the behavior of many religious sects. Examples such as the Waco siege and the Jonestown massacre show how a charismatic-style relationship can cause the disciples to behave in an apparently irrational manner, as judged by an objective onlooker.

Charismatic-style relationships also exist in less ex-

Figure 7.6
The charismatic-style relationship

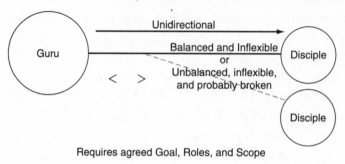

Relationship Weights vary—the guru has the control as long as the disciple maintains "faith."

Requires agreed Goal, Roles, and Scope

treme situations. Powerful leaders in any field can generate the same type of relationships. When this occurs the goals of the guru tend to take precedence over the normal operational decisions that the disciple might otherwise make. This may result in a positive or negative outcome. A guru, to operate successfully over time, must forget his powerful position and address the realities of everyday operation.

A positive example of a charismatic-style relationship is the Body Shop franchise chain. The Body Shop was the first cosmetics company to focus heavily on simple cosmetics made in ecologically friendly ways. The Body Shop is run by a guru-type figure, Anita Roddick. Her goals of safer, more ecologically sound products and the promotion of "trade not aid" guide the actions of those working in the Body Shop supply and franchise operations. The whole organization has a characteristic mode of operation defined by those shared values and beliefs. However, those driving social beliefs have to operate in an environment that enforces the discipline of the market. Therefore, the overall Relationship Style of the Body Shop, while charismatic, must also support the profile of a market-style relationship. In this example the charismatic-style relationship has created a positive result that appears to respond effectively in both the economic and social marketplace.

A negative example is the City Council of Liverpool, England, in the 1970s and 1980s. The Militant Tendency (a left-wing pressure group) took control of the Liverpool City Council. The guru figure was Derek Hatton. Charismatic-style relationships were promoted within the City Council. Interactions between council officials and employees became focused on the goals of the guru, and any challenges were taken very personally. Information about the operation of the council was restricted, resulting in esoteric operation. The control dimension came into play and dominated the operation dimension. For example, the guru-style leadership felt that their political goals were more important than the jobs of the council employees and the services provided to the local population. As a result, many jobs were lost and services were cut drastically. In the end a charismatic-style relationship becomes untenable if it does not produce an effective operational outcome. In this case the local council was audited by the local government auditors, and a number of local council members were found to be grossly negligent.

These two examples show both the power and the danger of charismatic-style relationships. They provide enormous focused energy on the shared goals, but they can easily become divorced from the reality of effective outcomes.

USING RELATIONSHIP STYLES

Relationship Styles provide a rapid response capability for understanding the interactions between entities. This capability is powerful because the Relationship Style identifies the likely behavior of both parties in a relationship. They uncover the overall style that an entity uses in building and operating relationships. Many problems that are encountered in relationships are the result of a conflict between these styles and the goals that each entity has in a relationship. Where such conflicts occur it is often difficult to unravel the problems. Relationship Styles enable a fast appreciation of the underlying dynamics of a relationship.

Many situations involve a mix of Relationship Styles. The example of the Body Shop showed a mixture of Charismatic and Market styles. In that example, the mix works well because the mix is made clear and everyone interacting with the Body Shop knows about the mix of styles. Other situations where a mix of styles occurs may cause problems. The example of the Citizen's Charter requires that the government mix Bureaucratic and Market styles together. Where that mix of styles occurs it creates opportunities for the participating entities to claim to be operating in one style when their main style is another. This can have a great effect on a relationship because all of us commonly use expected Relationship Styles to tailor our responses to other entities in relationships. This is particularly problematic when bureaucratic relationships are involved, because of their focus on control. When this clash of styles happens, the interaction that is generated around the relationship becomes confusing. The result of this confusion is that each entity seems to see any problems in a different way. Each entity tends to deny the view of the other, and that makes it difficult to identify the real cause of any problem and the potential for its resolution.

Relationships are influenced by the perceptions of the entities involved and a series of wider Relationship Influences and Styles. These affect the way in which relationships are operated and reflect the relative influence of the different relationship dimensions. Relationship Styles provide a mechanism for quickly understanding the nature of any interaction between entities and managing relationships more effectively. They complement the more detailed information generated by the Relationship Analysis steps of scoping, alignment, and profiling by providing an intuitive overview understanding of relationships.

CHAPTER 8

ORGANIZATIONAL CHANGE

Over the last ten years there has been a fundamental change in how organizations and markets are operated. This change will continue filtering through organizations well into the twenty-first century. The changes are focused on the flattening of organizational hierarchies, the desire to respond to the customer, and the increasing pace of change in both the nature of the work that people do and the demands of the marketplace. In this chapter we will focus on examples from specific organizations of whom we have experience and from whom we will generalize to the wider organizational and economic environment.

Asea Brown Boveri (ABB) is a worldwide heavy engineering company (based in Europe) with a turnover of around $30 billion. It is made up of some 5,000 independent profit centers. Each of these is in effect a small-scale business. The corporate staff have to deal with the challenge of being just another potential supplier of services to each of the small operational units. The central training department, for example, must demonstrate to each unit why it should buy training from them and the benefits that will follow. ABB invests in training and wishes to provide excellent services that can be utilized by the business units to improve their skills and ultimately their market position. ABB will, however, only provide such training services as part of the corporate function if they are world-class services that can be provided on the basis of income generated by the business units.

ABB has focused on the development of tightly integrated teams and small operationally focused units. This fragmentation and removal of intervening layers is typical of those organizations that have responded to the challenges of faster design to market times and the increasing specificity and power of the customer. The challenge for this new style of organization is to maintain links that define its nature and culture and that enable the overall group of small operational units to move forward in concert. This creates major challenges for the corporate staff, who are responsible for ensuring that ABB remains competitive and profitable.

The large management consultancies such as Arthur Andersen, KPMG, and McKinsey provide people and skills in a flexible mix that can be tailored to the needs of any specific customer. Their basic approach to business is to identify opportunities in the marketplace and then react based on highly flexible processes and highly skilled people. Behind this flexibility is a requirement to continuously form and reform relationships with many colleagues. Each project they take on may well involve different team members applying different skills in different situations. This continuous change requires that the consultants focus on their abilities to develop relationships with their customers and colleagues. Their opportunity to deploy their skills in any particular field, such as corporate finance, I.T. strategy, or human resource development, is totally dependent on their ability to form and maintain relationships in high-pressure situations.

Large consultancies and services organizations attempt to manage their customers in a two-pronged fashion. They provide account, or relationship, managers who develop long-term links with the customers' decision makers. They also provide experts in specific services who deliver the results that the customer wishes to see. This dual relationship is sometimes a difficult one to manage. The pressure on suppliers to provide high-quality skills and services often means that the individuals who can deliver the solutions are thinly spread and cannot develop a long-term relationship with the customer. This makes it difficult for the customer to develop confidence in the consultant and build a long-term relationship with the direct source of the expertise.

The account manager role has developed in an attempt to fill this gap. Account managers perform a much wider role than salesmen. They become problem solvers for the customer, attempting to provide an integration between supplier and customer and to smooth over problems of integration into each other's business processes. The difficulty with this two-pronged approach is that the relationship with the account manager is an enabling one rather than a delivery one. The enabling role is essentially serving two masters and can become confused. A potential solution to this problem is for organizations to deliberately develop partnerships based on trust, which removes the need for duplication or validation processes. The difficulty with this approach is that the links required to generate such a partnership will often make it difficult for other suppliers to break through, resulting in the customer not getting the best solution available. Another solution is to focus heavily on the relationship between the delivery consultant and the customer, either as an addition to the account manager role or in its place. By developing the delivery consultant's awareness of the nature of the relationship and its importance, a stronger bond can be created based on the customer-deliverer relationship. There is no one easy solution to this problem, but a focus on the nature of the relationships being built between the customer and supplier or the partners is key to managing such relationships effectively.

Hewlett-Packard (HP) is the only major success story of the early 1990s from the large computer system manufacturers who dominated the 1980s. In the 1980s IBM extended their position of dominance in the market for large computers, known as mainframes, and at the same time became the world's largest and most successful supplier of midrange systems with the AS400, and of small personal computers with the IBM PC. Digital Equipment Corporation (DEC) dominated the other midrange manufacturers with Hewlett-Packard, Data General, Wang, NCR, and AT&T following along behind. Of these companies only Hewlett-Packard has seen major growth in the 1990s. HP has grown from an annual turnover of around $10 billion in 1990 to around $30 billion in 1995; during this time they managed to invest some 10 percent of turnover in research and development and maintain profitability levels of some 5 to 10 percent, at a time when all of the other traditional manufacturers around them where experiencing large losses. How did they achieve this? They achieved it by a combination of superior technology, luck, and a focus on the development and management of internal and external relationships.

A well known approach to effective management, "Management by Wandering Around" (MBWA), originated at HP as part of the overall approach to management known as "The HP Way." MBWA is a simple approach to management, based on the principle that you should spend your time interacting with the people who are producing the products or services, not remain in an isolated ivory tower. The policy is all pervasive. A colleague at Hewlett-Packard in England decided to test the policy when he first visited the headquarters in Silicon Valley, soon after joining the company as a very junior employee. He walked into the area where Dave Packard, the head of the company, was usually to be found (at HP many executives and managers do not have offices as such, just somewhere they use as a base) and had a discussion with him about issues that he felt needed addressing within the company. This approach underpins the fundamental beliefs and organization of HP. The two founders, Dave Packard and Bill Hewlett, were engineers who firmly believed in local control, accountability, and small-scale operation. When a part of the company grew beyond direct control of its management, it was split off into a relatively autonomous division. This resulted in a continual focus on the operational elements of each division rather than an abstraction into corporate infighting.

In the late 1980s HP began to have serious problems. The previous focus on the individual had begun to be eroded, and the desire for an overall corporate identity had caused the proliferation of committees that considered issues affecting more than one division. As a result, it took six months to a year to get even small design issues agreed upon by the committees, at a time when the market required decisions to be made within weeks if not days. These problems were similar to those that IBM has been struggling to address over the previous five years. However, HP had an ace up its sleeve. Bill Hewlett and Dave Packard, although no longer involved in the day-to-day running of the company, decided they had to intervene. They made it clear to the management team that the key principles of individual responsibility and local accountability were being lost and this was threatening the whole company. As a result the focus for control was returned to the product divisions and the overbearing corporate committees removed.

This change was not easy. As organizations grow they build integration structures that help them to maintain their identity. IBM had grown so large and had such a high degree of internal control that it could not be removed easily without threatening the whole structure of the organization. HP, however, has a much freer culture. The employees had become alarmed at the stagnation of the organization, and were all for the changes that were made to free it up. The culture inside HP has always been an entrepreneurial one. This culture enabled the internal relationships in HP to withstand the pressure of change through the 1990s as the company had to reinvent its skills base and tackle new markets.

Hewlett-Packard has always focused on the development of partnerships. Although it has sometimes played the role of the overbearing giant, it has been able to develop key partnerships with external organizations. The main success story here is the partnership with Canon. The Japanese company produces the printer engines for HP's wildly successful LaserJet range of printers. HP is the world's Number One supplier of laser printers, using base technology that it licensed from Canon. Also, HP has recently entered a partnership with Intel, the world leader in PC microprocessors, to produce the next generation of microprocessors. This partnership could be as important to HP as the current one with Canon. What these partnerships show is HP's ability to work together with other organizations on a mutually profitable basis. The internal culture of HP has been crucial in enabling its development of successful external partnerships. (The partnerships mentioned above are but two of the many partnerships that HP maintains.) The focus on effective decision making, accountability at the point of delivery, and freedom to develop new solutions provides a culture that is predisposed to working with others.

IBM was the giant of the computer industry from 1970–90; it dominated all sectors of the market and was one of the world's most admired corporations. But over the last five years it sustained huge losses and produced virtually no market growth. Over the same period Hewlett-Packard has grown its turnover by more than 200 percent. How did this happen? Part of the problem was the high profitability of the large mainframe systems, which generated 40 percent plus profits, while the rest of the market produced only 5 to 10 percent profits. This overreliance on a dwindling market where the profit margins were also being slashed was a major problem.

Another major problem was their internal and external relationships. Internally they had built up a culture that appeared to all of their employees as a benevolent family. A job in IBM had traditionally been a job for life, and the huge profits generated by mainframe computer sales enabled an incredible package of benefits for the employees. Even in today's economic environment, IBM still provides such benefits as free summer camps for the children of managers.

This culture produced great benefits when the company was profitable, by creating an organization that dressed, worked, and played with one mind. In contrast, HP's culture had always been entrepreneurial. Many employees at Hewlett-Packard saw it as a staging post in their career, and were encouraged to do so by the organization. As a result, when changes in manning levels and skills were required in the early 1990s, the culture shock at HP was relatively small. But at IBM the family culture was torn apart by the changes and involved hundreds of thousands of jobs lost. The IBM organization had always provided control and security in its employees' lives; in return for this the employees provided hard work and loyalty. The increasing pace of change and substitutability of products in the computer industry has broken apart this cozy corporate family structure, because competition is now possible on all fronts. Small competitors can enter the market with innovative and flexible products and services that challenge the once impregnable economies of scale and the cozy executive-level relationships of the corporate giants. Each part of an organization now has to contribute directly to the bottom line. The increase in competition and the availability of competing products and services means that the customer no longer has to pay for the social and personal benefits previously provided by the large corporations for their employees; he can buy a cheaper product from a smaller competitor. The high levels of overhead merely make companies like IBM uncompetitive and threaten their employees' jobs. IBM's internal relationships have suffered dramatic change, and even now some employees still believe the old approach can return.

Fundamental to these changes is the shift from corporate responsibility and performance to personal responsibility and performance. The development of information technology and the wide availability of a flexible contract-based manufacturing capability have changed the nature of corporate assets. The old corporate approach to appraising assets was to identify the fixed asset value of the organization and add on the market position in terms of good will and financial performance. Now many companies are springing up with virtually no fixed assets, just the skill of their employees. Even heavy manufacturing firms such as ABB will contract out for much of their product and services. Less than 5 percent of ABB's total sales-to-delivery cycle time involves manufacturing. This creates a change in the nature of the asset value of an organization. It becomes the skills of its people that determine the performance and ultimately the value of an organization, rather than the fixed assets the organization could previously directly control. People are not fixed and can move on. The organization does not own them in the same way as it owns a piece of machinery. This makes a modern organization a much more fluid and flexible animal. It also changes the nature of the contract between a company and its employees. The massive increase in the number of consultancies reflects this fact. When an employee has a high level of skill that the market desires, it is very easy for that employee to satisfy the market directly by becoming independent.

The proliferation of such flexible services in the marketplace has resulted in a general desire for increased performance and flexibility from all organizations. IBM has had to remove the protective cover from its employees and expose them to the realities of the market. They have found this very difficult and have suffered over the last five years as a direct result.

IBM tended to operate its external relationships in a similar manner. It was always looking to control any "partner-ships" with other companies. It felt that other organizations should be grateful to work with IBM and it always attempted to gain formal control over a relationship. When IBM dealt with a small company, it would insist that the small company sign non-disclosure agreements about everything before dis-cussion would begin. They would, however, resist signing any parallel agreements about disclosure of the other com-pany's secrets. This was part of the price to be paid if a small company wanted to come under the benevolent wing of IBM.

Internally IBM had many layers of legal controls. The top layer was a corporate practices department that reported back to headquarters about the activities of the divisions. In ABB the corporate staff rarely have to resolve conflicts be-tween the operating companies. It is expected that the oper-ating companies involved will deal with any issues them-selves and that if they cannot, those responsible will not remain in the company for long. But at IBM the "Manage-ment Committee" was all powerful. Any conflicts would be bucked up through the system and resolved at the highest level. This made for slow and removed decision making. Po-litical considerations operate at this level in organizations, and the focus is often on bureaucratic control and structure rather than the operational imperatives. As the market changed over the 1990s this approach became untenable.

A good example of this can be seen in the operating divi-sions that IBM has sold. Many of these are now performing as thriving businesses with much lower costs and higher profits. In many of these operations the move to indepen-dence involved a removal of the IBM "family" approach. The printer and typewriter divisions became a company called Lexmark.

All the changes happening at once upset a lot of people in Lexington. One likened IBM's decision to sell to the situation of someone who came home to find his wife wanted to divorce him. Even though he might have known the divorce was coming, it was still tough to be kicked out. Another said he knew that IBM had tried hard to make the sale go well and to make sure that Lexmark would take good care of the former IBMers but, he said, that IBM was still like a father who took his young son for a walk, took him up to a strange house, and said "Son, this house is equivalent to ours and this man and this woman here will be equivalent parents. So I'll leave you here now. Goodbye.

Paul Carroll, *Big Blues: The Unmaking of IBM* (London: Orion Books, 1993)

As shown in the above quotation, the changes that Lexmark made were not easy. They slashed overheads, gave those who build their printers and typewriters responsibility, authority, and accountability, and focused on developing relationships with their sales agents and corporate customers. As a result, they are now much more technically innovative, they have introduced the first low cost 1200dpi laser printer, and they have focused on their specific market. The nature of their internal and external relationships has changed dramatically. IBM is still struggling to turn itself around. It has returned to profit, but is no longer the all-powerful giant it once was. It is having to deal with other organizations on a more equal basis, but is still suffering from its inability to move with the speed of its competitors.

The nature of operation of organizations is changing. The great manufacturing industries thrive on a combination of automation and economies of scale. Such industries required a well-defined sequence of operations to be performed many times to produce a given output. Through the large scale of its operation costs could be minimized and profits maximized. This resulted in a heavily controlled bureaucratic form of operation. The focus was on reducing error and variation and optimizing the operation of the automated process. In order to reach this goal a reductionist approach was developed, with each element of an organization being given its own specific performance objectives. The result was a focus on the structure and control elements of an organization. IBM spent much of its senior management's time checking that the organization was operating according to the corporate directives. This focus on control and structure, derived from their past success, has been their great Achilles' heel.

The basic dynamic of social and economic life is changing. The era of industrialization is being superseded by the era of the information, or knowledge-based, society. This has two major effects. Consumers are able to make educated choices about the products and services that they wish to purchase. No longer will they settle for a limited choice, or buy merely because they have bought that product before. The increased capability of automation and computerization has reduced the advantages of economies of scale. Speed of response to changing customer needs requires flexible systems and people, rather than highly efficient giant processes that respond slowly. The notion of "added value" has become all powerful. We no longer buy simple products; we buy image, opportunity, and promise. The industrialized societies have created wealth that far exceeds the basic needs of their people to survive. This has caused a shift in the nature of the power and control in Western society, and organizations have had to respond to that shift by changing the nature of their operation. The individual has become more powerful, because the key element in the means of production is changing from the ownership of natural or manufactured resources to the knowledge and expertise of each individual or group.

The organizations identified above show how this change is impacting. Hewlett-Packard and the big six consultancies have always focused on the capability of their individuals and groups. As a result, they have been able to adjust their organizational structure and control mechanisms to cope with the increasing focus on knowledge and information. ABB, a group of traditional manufacturing companies, made a fundamental change by tearing out the overbearing control structures and passing control to the small operational units. IBM found it extremely difficult to change. A major impediment was the expectations and emotional perspective of their employees. Their great strength in the past was the development of a family culture, in which employees were happy to be moved around and respond to requests because IBM always looked after them. IBM used to move its employees around so much that there is an old joke about IBM's name, that it stood for "I've Been Moved." In building this culture, a foundation of centralized accountability and decision making was established, which left most employees to follow what was decided rather than making decisions and taking risks themselves. It is this culture that is causing IBM so many problems today.

The rise of individual or group accountability is based on this change in capability. As individuals become more important to the operation of an organization, so their rewards are more directly related to their performance. The rise in performance- and profit-related pay, short-term contracts, and project-focused operation reflects this. Organizations are having to remove control structures and rely on the capability of their employees, partners, and suppliers to deliver the required results. As the emphasis moves from the organization to the capability of its people, the protection of the organization for its people gradually reduces. No longer are customers prepared to pay for high corporate overheads, because there are many alternatives for them in the marketplace. As products become more highly valued for their image, information content, and personal impact, there is much greater scope for alternatives to be developed. Further, the ability of large organizations to protect their employees was, in the past, based on their control of markets and the ability to generate long-running stable revenues from products. But increase in the pace of change and reduction in the market control of large organizations has resulted in large organizations losing the ability to create long-running stable environments for their employees. This is the exact problem at IBM. The loss of this stable base of products and income is forcing organizations to change. Those that refuse are finding it increasingly difficult to survive.

These changes are occurring most slowly in the governmental or publicly funded organizations. Such organizations focus on performing according to political direction and/or statute. As such they are not directly accountable to their "customers" for the manner of their operation. A further problem is that governmental and public organizations are the essence of bureaucracies.

They must have defined modes of operation because they have to be seen to operate in a legal and proper manner. They often become focused on the nature of that operation rather than the outcomes that they generate. In fact their relatively fixed bureaucratic structures often make it difficult to generate the outcomes that they wish to achieve.

Another problem with these organizations is their link to political power and their tendency to prosecute political agendas rather than focus on the desired outcomes. This creates a conflict in the nature of the accountability and responsibility that they have. They can claim to be accountable to those that elected them or set them up, but in reality they often act as if accountable to a political dogma. They often accept that they are responsible for taking action but then deny accountability for the specific outcomes of that action. This approach is justified on the basis that they are people performing a public service and are often not able to defend themselves in public. The attempts to open up these organizations have focused on the creation of customer charters and defined performance levels. The problem in creating real accountability is that there is no direct customer response (unlike the open market where customers can stop buying a product and service) to generate the fast responses now required in the private sector. There is no easy solution that can be applied to these public bureaucracies. Their nature requires a larger degree of control and stability than private organizations. It is in the opening up of their operation that the best path lies so that the necessary structure and bureaucratic mode of operation becomes clear and well understood.

All of these examples show how the nature of the relationships between people and organizations has a critical effect on the effectiveness of those relationships. In the examples, we have begun to uncover the key dimensions and elements in the operation of organizations, groups, and people and seen how organizations are having to change to a more open, accountable, and simple mode of operation. These concepts are the foundation of Relationship Dynamics. Relationship Dynamics identifies the key dimensions and elements that affect the way in which we all operate and interact in the social and economic environment.

CHAPTER 9

APPLYING
RELATIONSHIP DYNAMICS

As you have seen in the previous chapters, Relationship Dynamics provides an understanding of the basic mechanism of social and economic action. As such it obviously applies to most of the situations that we encounter in life. This chapter will look at four specific areas of applications of relationship theory. Each of these areas could be the subject of a book in its own right, so this chapter will provide a taste of how Relationship Dynamics applies to it. The four areas are

- The operation of organizations and their culture
- The optimization of processes
- The extension of systems analysis into the relationship dimension
- Widening corporate strategy

THE OPERATION OF ORGANIZATIONS AND THEIR CULTURE

Relationships, within organizations and between organizations, operate from different perspectives. Relationship Dynamics provides the mechanism to understand both of these different forms of relationship. The internal operation of an organization is determined by:

- the goals of the organization
- the culture of the organization
- the actions that the organization and its component entities take to achieve those goals within that culture
- the structure of management and control set up to direct the operation of the organization

The goals of an organization determine the nature of the internal operation of that organization and the exchanges it enters into. The homeostatic goals may range from the maximization of profit to the basic maintenance of the organization. The culture of an organization is represented by the customs and values that are generated within it. The impact of that culture is most powerfully seen in the manner in which an organization forms and maintains both its internal and external relationships. Relationship Analysis provides a technique to identify the goals and culture of an organization in terms of the desired relationships and their desired profiles. These internal relationship profiles provide an effective and powerful representation of the nature of the interactions that the members of an organization engage in and the values that they subscribe to.

For example, the relationship profile identifies the levels of bonding, trust, respect, and approval that operate within an organization. It also identifies the manner in which interactions are operated in terms of their openness, flexibility, and formality. The relationship profile provides a clear picture of the intangible but powerful aspects that create the intuitively experienced environment of the organization. This intuitively experienced environment is extremely powerful in determining how well new members of an organization adjust to the expected manner of operation. It also has a major impact on potential customers and partners; this intuitive experience is a powerful element in the degree to which others approve of and wish to interact with that organization.

The control structure of the organization provides the mechanism for the organization to operate in a prescribed manner, generating feedback from the operational element to the management and control elements. The nature of the control structure will vary among organizations and will contribute to the cultural identity of each organization. For example, if an organization has a highly bureaucratic style of management, the interaction between employees will be highly formal and prescribed. If the organization has a partnership style of management, the need for high-level control is reduced and the interactions between employees will be characterized by peer-to-peer interaction rather than manager-to-subordinate interaction.

Internally, an organization involves people and other resources in the operation of processes to generate products and/or services. Relationships are created and information exchanged to enable the processes to work. The products and services produced are then used to generate income for the organization and its members, through external relationships with other organizations and individuals. The exact nature of these external relationships, which usually operate on the basis of a market-based exchange or one of the relationship styles identified previously, is determined by the participating entities.

In analyzing the operation of an organization it is important to understand all of the contributing influences. To achieve this, a series of relatively standard analytical techniques have been developed over the last forty years, including:

- skills analysis, personality analysis, and performance analysis—to analyze people
- product quality analysis, performance analysis—to analyze products
- resource quality analysis, performance analysis—to analyze resources
- process modeling, quality management, and process reengineering—to analyze processes
- Information Engineering, Entity Relationship Analysis, and Information Flow Analysis—to analyze information

Before the development of Relationship Dynamics there was no systematic way of identifying, capturing, and analyzing the essential nature of the relationships between entities inside organizations. Relationship Dynamics provides this additional awareness and understanding. The importance of relationships is increasing as organizations become more dependent on their workers' knowledge, and the manner in which they operate and interact with their suppliers and customers. Many organizations differentiate themselves not on the basis of their products, but by the manner in which they can provide and service them. Organizations operate through relationships. Relationships are the oil that lubricates their operation.

While those more established analytical techniques, identified above, provide some understanding of the relationships that sit around their focus of analysis, they rarely bring out the full issues. Nor do they provide a model for understanding the impact of relationship changes or indicating how the changes could be successfully managed. This is particularly the case for the understanding of individual behavior. Static models of people with specific personalities, skills, and competencies are often used, but the real world is not static; rather, it is a dynamic environment in which people interact with each other and with other entities. Thus it is the dynamic formation and operation of relationships that provides the most effective understanding of the impact of change on individuals inside organizations. Relationship Dynamics also provides the concept of entity, control, or process focus for the analysis of relationships. This enables the internal interactions within an organization to be evaluated from the appropriate perspective and allows the competing influences to be separated for examination and possible change.

THE OPTIMIZATION OF PROCESSES

> If process innovation is to succeed, the human side of change cannot be left to manage itself. Organizational and Human Resource issues are more central than technology issues to the behavioural changes that must occur within a process.
>
> Thomas H. Davenport, *Process Innovation: Reengineering Work Through Information Technology* (Cambridge, MA: Harvard Business School Press, 1993)

A business process is the collection of activities that are required to take a customer request and generate the required output for that customer. The characteristic approach to business processes, since the beginning of the Industrial Revolution, has been to break such processes up into simple tasks and generate specialist skills, tools, and knowledge for each task. The result of this approach is to provide optimal performance for each individual task, but unfortunately the overall objective, that of meeting the customer request, is often forgotten. As this specialization became endemic, organizations created separate departments, which defined their own goals and often created barriers between themselves and other departments. With the increasing competition and pace of change generated in the 1980s and 1990s three problems began to emerge:

- Organizations began to find that the overhead resulting from each department having its own goals and procedures, together with the barriers to passing work from one department to another, was causing great inefficiencies.
- The individuals within these departmental and task boundaries had skills that only applied to a small part of the customer-focused process and would only take responsibility for their element of work. This made it impossible to identify the responsibility and accountability for the overall customer-focused process because it was too fragmented.
- The manner in which work was carried out had become defensive and power focused around the department and task boundaries. The relationships needed to focus on the overall goal of meeting customer need could therefore not be established.

This created a fundamental questioning of the classic organization model. From this questioning a new view of the nature of operation of organizations has taken hold—the process view. This change, from a task view of operation to a process view, requires challenging both the existing departmental and task structures of organizations and the boundaries that individuals have created for themselves within these structures.

The ability to form and maintain relationships is a skill that enables people to operate effectively in many situations. As people and the environment around them change, so will their relationships. While processes are statements of steps that will transform a customer request into an effective response, relationships are the oil that lubricates those processes. It is possible to identify an effective process for a business situation as a static statement of possible interactions between people, machines, and business tasks. At any point in time the best process can be identified. Relationships, however, being interactions between entities that operate at many levels, vary continuously. Effective understanding of relationships provides a mechanism for controlling and steering an organization, whatever the processes being operated.

Relationship management can be thought of as the equivalent of a dynamic control center. A car has a steering wheel, accelerator, brake, and gearbox. These are continuously adjusted and changed to enable the car to move effectively through its environment. The ability of entities to form and manage relationships provides a similar ongoing capability that can be applied to adjust the manner in which processes are operated.

There are currently many different approaches to the understanding and improvement of business processes. In the literature on all of these approaches, the importance of managing the relationships that service these processes is identified. There is, however, little practical advice on the theories and techniques that can be used to understand and respond to these interactive human elements. This lack of direct advice on how to address these issues leaves many process-improvement initiatives with difficulties.

For example, a major U.S. industrial company has carried out reengineering exercises that have not delivered the returns expected. A newly engineered process that was theoretically capable of being operated in two weeks took three weeks to complete. The process was viewed by the organization as a mechanistic one that happened to involve people. The inability of the workforce to operate the process as designed was seen as a failure by the workforce as individuals. This led to individuals being evaluated for performance by the Human Resources Department and told to change the way they behaved. No real assistance in understanding the dynamics of the changing relationships they had encountered was provided.

In fact, the problem was due to the change in the relationships that the workforce had to form in order to operate the new process. They were required to interact differently, taking on different degrees of accountability, responsibility, trust, etc. These types of change have a major impact on the way that people work. To be managed effectively, such changes must be identified and planned for as part of the process of change.

Process improvement involves an incremental approach to improving business processes. The goal is to generate small but sustained improvements in existing business process. One of the main vehicles for process improvements in organizations is Total Quality Management (TQM). TQM applies traditional statistical techniques to the analysis of specific business processes or process elements. From this analysis, the overall performance and the variability of performance can be identified. Various strategies and tactics can then be applied to addressing the performance and variability issues identified. This approach to process improvement is aimed at generating continual small improvements over the lifetime of a business process. It does not usually involve questioning the whole foundation of a business process. The analysis tools used provide useful information about other types of process, but do not capture many of the key elements of the relationships required to facilitate the operation of business processes.

Business Process Reengineering (BPR) is an approach to the design of business processes that has been heavily promoted in the early 1990s. Its two key concepts are these:

- Organizations should take a fresh look at their business processes and design new processes from scratch. In doing so, existing organizational boundaries should be ignored.
- Business processes should begin with an initial request for action (from a customer or internal source) and integrate all tasks through to the requester's receipt of the product or service. The focus should be on identifying the sequence of operations that make up these request-focused business processes and their optimization.

The process of reengineering a business is not, in itself, revolutionary. Rather, the willingness to attempt it requires that the organization be prepared to initiate and manage a potential revolution in the manner in which it operates, both internally and externally. The tools used for BPR are not necessarily new. Many existing process definition and analysis tools can be applied to the design/redesign of new and existing business processes.

Work flow refers to the passage of work through a business process. A business process involves the allocation of tasks to people. Workflow facilitates that allocation of tasks and also provides a mechanism for monitoring the progress of the tasks within a business process. One of the requirements of an effective business process is that the flow and allocation of work introduce minimal delay to the process.

Work flow has been heavily promoted as a new information technology that can apply computing solutions to this allocation and flow of work. Sophisticated computer systems can automate the flow of work through a business process, and can provide an overview of the efficiency of that process and those operating it. Work flow is, therefore, a tool that can be applied within either a process improvement or a process reengineering exercise. Work flow can be seen as providing two contributions to process analysis and improvement:

- Analysis techniques for identifying the flow of work through a business process
- Software tools and solutions that provide the ability to automate the allocation, flow, and management of work through a defined business process

Relationships are the mechanism by which people interact effectively with other people in the operation of a business process. Business processes are dependent on having

- people with the appropriate skills
- resources and techniques to support effective operation
- effective relationships between the people operating the business process

Most approaches to process reengineering address the

first two issues above but very few address the third issue. Mike Hammer, the original guru of BPR, identifies many changes generated when redesigning business processes, including the following.

- Several jobs become combined into one.
- Workers make decisions.
- Checks and controls are reduced.
- Jobs change from simple tasks to multidimensional ones.
- People's roles change from controlled to empowered.
- Job preparation changes from training to education.
- Advancement criteria change from performance to overall ability.
- Values change from protective to productive.
- Managers change from supervisors to coaches.
- Organizational structures change from hierarchical to flat.

These changes impact not only on the processes an organization operates but also on the capability of their employees and the environment of command and control. Most approaches to the redesign of business processes tend to focus on the mechanistic elements of process change rather than on the people and relationship issues of process change.

The tools and techniques used to reengineer organizations have been developed from systems analysis tools and focus on the graphic representation of processes and the flow of information between them. The toolkits and the techniques that go with them focus on a mechanistic approach to process redesign, whereby a new optimal set of tasks is identified within a customer-focused business process. There is little information gathered on the manner in which the new business processes will be operated, nor is

Figure 9.1
Process before reengineering

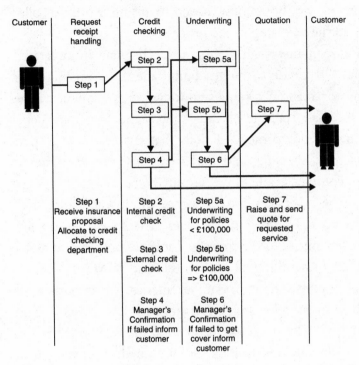

Customer	Request receipt handling	Credit checking	Underwriting	Quotation	Customer

	Step 1	Step 2	Step 5a		
		Step 3	Step 5b	Step 7	
		Step 4	Step 6		

	Step 1 Receive insurance proposal Allocate to credit checking department	Step 2 Internal credit check	Step 5a Underwriting for policies < £100,000	Step 7 Raise and send quote for requested service
		Step 3 External credit check	Step 5b Underwriting for policies => £100,000	
		Step 4 Manager's Confirmation If failed inform customer	Step 6 Manager's Confirmation If failed to get cover inform customer	

contrasting information gathered about the manner in which the previous business processes were operated.

These changes impact directly on those required to implement redesigned business processes. The implementation of new business processes must address these issues directly. Many organizations have found that their failure to do so has compromised the effectiveness of the new processes. Identifying the potential relationship issues and then addressing them is not a complex process. It can be achieved incrementally with the existing techniques and tools.

Figures 9.1 and 9.2 show a process before and after reengineering. Prior to reengineering the process involved seven steps, including management checking. The customer request was moved among four departments. Responsibility for processing the request moved each time work was allocated to the next step in the process.

After reengineering the process has become an integrated whole, with no departmental boundaries. Responsibility for taking the customer request through each element of the process is allocated to an integrated team. The team members have a broad range of skills that enables them to perform credit checking and underwriting for most requests. When complex evaluation is required, specialist services are used. These services must operate within the parameters agreed upon by the process team. The specialists do not take over control of the process. Tools are provided to assist the team in handling all of the tasks and providing fast, effective responses to any customer queries. The process itself can be evaluated for the performance of all requests that go through it. This enables the organization to manage the process directly and to look for continued improvement of operation.

A reengineered process generates a major change in the relationships that the members of a process team have to form. Managing this change and the ongoing operation of these relationships is a critical requirement in the successful implementation of the new business process.

A failure to identify the relationship element of new business processes has led to many organizations encountering problems. New processes may often appear cleaner, simpler, and more direct, but they may not operate in the expected manner. With the reengineered process shown in Figure 9.2, individuals may find the following:

Figure 9.2
Process after reengineering

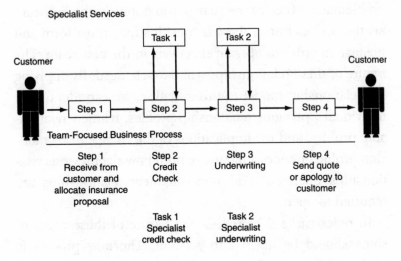

- The department that they were part of disappears. This results in a removal of previous informal support structures, which now need to be rebuilt from scratch.
- The skills that were learned to a large degree by working alongside those more experienced in the same area are now threatened, because they are located in a team that has no other members with those extended skills. The mechanism for personal skill development has therefore been removed.
- The values of other team members are different from the values held by their previous department.
- Team members are required to change their skill sets.
- Team members become accountable for actions that previously they were not accountable for.

The traditional response to managing these changes has been to focus on new skills training and the individual's ability to work in a team. While the new skills issue is important, the focus on individuals rather than relationships is problematic. Much of the change will not be in the individuals themselves but in the relationships they must form and manage in order to operate effectively in the new team. The nature of these relationships will have changed. By applying the relationship model to this situation, we can identify an individual's previous relationship profiles, his new relationship profiles, and the implications of the change. A relationship profile provides a picture of both how the previous relationships operated, and how the new relationships are required to operate.

In redesigning the process, the nature of these relationships should be taken into account. The new process is likely to require the formation of both new relationships and new types of relationships. The traditional process reengineering view of the key elements of a business system, are characterized by the "business system diamond" associated with CSC Index and Hammer and Company. This identifies the four points of a business system diamond. This diamond is supposed to identify everything about the company. It provides a view of

- the business processes, with their integral tasks
- the jobs and structures required to operate those business processes; from this the skills and capabilities of people to operate those processes can be identified, as can the nature of the teams
- the management and measurement systems that oversee and structure the business processes
- the employees' and the organization's values and beliefs.

All four points of the business system diamond have to fit

together or the company will be flawed and misshapen. In this view of a business there is a focus on each business process, the tasks it comprises, and how those tasks are linked together. We should be able to derive the roles that must operate to perform the tasks and how the people performing these roles link together. There is, however, little focus on the manner of these interactions between people, nor on the impact that the operation of these relationships can have on the success of the new business processes. We believe that the business system diamond must be extended to include the relationships that must be formed between people to operate these new business processes more effectively.

Adding the relationship dimension to a business process analysis exercise is relatively simple. A full scale Relationship Analysis can be carried out to provide a new perspective on the operation of the process and an overview of the issues that the new business process will need to address. The output from this full-scale analysis can then be used as an input to the standard business process analysis tools. The results from both analysis processes would then be used in the design, implementation, and management of the new business process.

Alternatively, the business process analysis will produce information about the interactions between people. These interactions can be used to identify and evaluate both the alignment of goals, roles, and scope and the Relationship Profile.

This approach enables organizations that have already started on a traditional process analysis and redesign exercise to easily extend their analysis and response to include the relationship elements that are crucial in the effective design and implementation of business process.

THE EXTENSION OF SYSTEMS ANALYSIS INTO THE RELATIONSHIP DIMENSION

The traditional approach used in analyzing manual or automated systems is known as Organization and Methods Analysis. This approach is derived from work-study techniques developed in the first half of the twentieth century. These techniques were focused on optimizing the performance of individuals providing manual input with an automated manufacturing system. In the 1960s and 1970s these methods were adapted and extended through integration with the approaches emerging from the computing environment. These approaches focus on a mechanistic and deterministic definition of processes and information rather than on the performance of individuals and groups within systems. Another branch of analysis, Human Factors Analysis, has also developed from the work-study techniques; it focuses on the impact of systems and technology on the individuals who operate systems. In the development of computer systems, while there may be a Human Factors Analysis of the physical impact of the interaction between physical system elements and the people who operate systems, it is rare for the overall set of relationships within the system to be evaluated. For example, when Microsoft develops a new word processor or spreadsheet, they will go through extensive usability design and testing. This will show how easy it is for a person to physically operate the computer system. There is, therefore, a focus on physical interaction with the system, but it is rare for the impact of the system that will contain that computer software tool to be evaluated for its impact on the overall system within which it will be used.

A computer system will usually comprise a series of separate components that require operation and linkage by people. Those people will interact with the computer system and other individuals, groups, or organizations in an overall social system aimed at generating a result. The overall system is subject to all of the relationship influences and pressures identified previously. The introduction of a new computer system may result in an individual having to perform new tasks, operate within a new control structure with fundamentally changed authority and responsibility levels, and interact with a new group of people. These impacts, also identified in the section above on process improvement, are often the elements that must be most carefully managed if change is to succeed. As a result, the successful implementation of a new computer system will be heavily dependent on the nature of the new relationship matrix within which it must operate.

In addition to this general requirement to plan for relationship change when developing systems, new developments in computer systems will make the relationship element even more crucial. The term *artificial intelligence* refers to the creation of a computer system that can operate such that its performance is indistinguishable from a human being. In the 1970s and early 1980s great strides were made in conceptual and practical development of artificial intelligence–based systems that could operate on the basis of rule systems and pattern analysis. However, during the 1980s these developments floundered when they encountered the problems of nondeterministic open systems referred to in Chapter 1. As attempts were made to scale artificial intelligence up and out of small-scale laboratory systems, the complexity of real-world application was found to be great. While there is still much good work being carried out in the artificial intelligence area, progress has become much slower.

In recent years a concept that was part of both artificial intelligence (where it was known as a *frame*) and more mainstream system development, that of an "object," has begun to take hold. An object can be considered as an entity. This means that it has an identity, a state, and behavior and can communicate with other objects through a series of interfaces. For example, a person can be considered an object. A person has an *identity*. We can uniquely identify a person from a number of indicators, such as his name, social security number, fingerprints, or dental records. We can therefore distinguish one person from another. A person has a *state*. At any one time a person has a weight, a height, a temperature, a geographical position in the world, etc. A person has *behavior*. We can speak, run, write, sing, fight, work, etc. A person can communicate with other people. We do this by a number of defined interfaces. We have visual, auditory, and touch based interfaces. These interfaces can receive different types of information, which we can decode and then act upon.

A computer software object has these same properties. It must have an *identity* so that it can be sent messages. It will have a *state*. This means that it can store information, such as an address or a company name, and the information stored reflects the current nature of that information. It has a series of interfaces. These receive a defined set of information in a format that the software object can understand. It has *behavior*. It can receive a message and carry out an action. For example, a calculator has a keyboard interface to capture information from the real world. When the keyboard is pressed, information is passed to a small computer program that understands the keystrokes and can perform the behavior of calculating a result from the numbers and operator indicated. The program can then initiate the display of the result on the calculator screen.

The calculator can also be seen as an object. It has *identity*. If you could not identify the calculator you could not use it, or you would not be sure that the calculator with the answer was the same one that you used to key in the calculation. It receives a message to perform a particular calculation with a specific set of numbers. It carries out the *behavior* of calculation and sends a message back via its screen. The calculator has a *state*. When you wish to perform a calculation the calculator must be reset to accept a new calculation. When it presents the result, it has changed its state from its "ready for a new calculation" to its "present result" state.

In the same way that a person is made up of component objects such as a brain, heart, or lungs, a calculator is made up of component objects, such as a keyboard, a display, and software. This concept of a component is crucial, because it indicates that entities can be built out of cooperative elements that together can be given identity. For example, a car is made up of an engine, a chassis, a gearbox, a braking system, etc. Each one of these elements or objects can perform on its own and can be replaced within the overall system.

Raising the concept to the level of a system, a system can be seen as the overall behavior generated by the objects within it and their interactions. We can now conceive of a system as a series of different types of objects such as people, computers, and machines interacting with each other. This therefore raises the question of what is the nature of the relationship that is generated between the objects involved in a system. When the components of a system were either people, who could act intelligently, or "machines" that merely provided manual assistance or calculation, it was possible to play down the importance of the nature of the relationship created between the different elements of the system. However, the reality is that powerful relationships have always been created between people and machines. A direct example is the car. Instead of thinking of a car as a physical machine, think of it as part of a "driving system" where the driver interacts with the car to create behavior that neither could achieve independently. This unity of purpose is one of the reasons why people do create powerful relationships with their cars. All of the relationship dimensions identified in Relationship Dynamics come into play in the relationship that many people have with their cars, including, paradoxically for a nonhuman entity, that most human element—bonding.

A new development in computer systems is the concept of the *intelligent agent*. These are software objects that have specific directed behavior and can "initiate action," or investigate the performance of other objects or systems, and report information back. For example, an intelligent agent might intercept all of your electronic mail, check who it is from, what its content is, and, on the basis of defined rules and past experience, prioritize and sort the mail so that you can read the important mail first. Another agent may send out pulses around a computer network, identify where any problems might occur, and raise alarms to warn the system operator. These intelligent agents are beginning to emerge and are performing tasks that were once performed by people. They will become part of the "relationship loop" that links people together. For example, a well-known technique in selling is to make sure that you build a positive relationship with the secretary of an important customer. It is this relationship, often built upon the emotion dimension, that can be the key element in generating access to the customer and the subsequent sale. In the near future the integration of voice-mail systems and intelligent agents could create a systems-based replacement for the "gatekeeper" role previously played by the secretary or personal assistant. This would change the whole nature of the relationships involved in the process of selling.

Therefore, it becomes even more important to view any system, manual, automated, or computerized, as a series of interactions between entities in the form of agents. New methods have been developed to provide the basis for such models. These methods enable the description of systems in terms of objects that combine to form systems and that interact with other systems that act as agents. Jacobson's Objectory and Hewlett-Packard's Fusion Object Oriented Analysis and Design methods are examples of these.

Figure 9.3 shows people interacting with systems or "automated agents." As this interaction becomes based on more human-like tasks, the nature of the connection between the person and the "system" becomes more of a relationship. For example, a scenario possible today is to have an automated agent on your PC that responds to voice control. In the morning you turn on your PC and speak to it. You might ask the agent (whom you may have called "Bill") to go and get any new electronic or voice mail and to send a message to a colleague to confirm a meeting to be held at 10.00 A.M. the next morning. This type of interaction starts to blur the difference between the person and the electronic agent in the "system" of the organization.

RELATIONSHIP DYNAMICS

Figure 9.3

Extending the system model

- The environment is defined as a group of communicating systems.
- A system is any type of system, software, hardware, or person/group, etc.
- A particular system "sees" all of the external system it interacts with as agents.

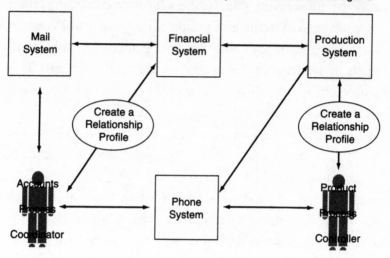

As these new developments become pervasive it is important to identify and manage the relationship issues that will develop. How will people react to these changes? Relationship Dynamics provides the mechanism to profile, understand, and analyze these relationships. It is likely that soon the analysis of relationships will become a key part of systems analysts' toolkit as they strive to create more effective systems.

WIDENING CORPORATE STRATEGY

Strategy is a plan of action, formulated in order to achieve specified objectives. After the objectives have been identified the problem, situation, or opportunity is examined and an evaluation made of the potential courses of action and their outcomes. In determining these courses of action and their outcomes many factors must be evaluated: economic, political, cultural, social, moral, and psychological factors. A major challenge for any process of strategy development is to capture and analyze effectively information about all of the influencing factors. This requires effective theories and models of analysis for each of the influencing factors. Traditional strategic analysis provides organizations with information on

- market structure
- the potential for development and profitability in a market
- the position of an organization in relation to the market and potential competitors
- the capability of that organization to operate in a market

This information is used to generate a picture of the future environment within which the organization will operate and to identify the most effective courses of action. The need to address economic, political, cultural, social, moral, and psychological factors, combined with an appreciation of both the deterministic and nondeterministic nature of the business environment, makes business-strategy formulation extremely difficult. Further, strategy focuses on what might happen in the future. Many of the techniques that are used to evaluate the business environment provide information about the past. But performance in the past does not necessarily indicate anything about future performance.

CURRENT APPROACHES TO STRATEGIC ANALYSIS

Current approaches to strategic analysis seek to provide an understanding of the nature of the competitive dynamic. These approaches include a number of analytical processes.

The standard analysis of industry structure is based on Michael Porter's structural analysis technique. This defines the key structural influences as being

- threats/barriers to entry
- threats of substitutes
- the power of suppliers
- the power of buyers
- competitive rivalry

This form of analysis provides information about an industry sector, based on the relative power of the organizations and individuals in it. The usual approach is to analyze demographic trends. The expected response of the organization and its competitors to these trends is then evaluated. This approach requires an element of crystal gazing. For example, in the late 1980s many competitive analyses identified the trend towards increasing home ownership and spending in Britain as leading to an expansion in out-of-town Do It Yourself (DIY) and furniture warehouse operations that attracted the younger home owners. This trend did not last, however, and the major businesses such as Queensway, Coloroll, Do It All, B&Q, and MFI either failed or had to be restructured. Maturity analysis is based on a basic life cycle of markets, which identifies a sequential development through the stages of

- development
- growth
- shakeout
- maturity
- decline

Different opportunities exist for an organization depending

on their position in the life cycle. A Critical Success Factor (CSF) analysis attempts to define the key issues that will affect an organization. A similar technique, called Strengths, Weaknesses, Opportunities, and Threats (SWOT) analysis, looks at the key issues identified in the environment and then analyzes them in terms of the organization's strengths and weaknesses. Strategic decisions are then facilitated by this understanding of the operation profile of the organization.

Value Chain Analysis is a technique identified by Michael Porter. It places the resource elements required to satisfy need into a chain. It identifies each element and the contribution that the element makes to adding value to the final product or service. The chain is not restricted to one organization; rather it stretches from the first identification of need through each contributing organization or individual until the need has been satisfied.

Porter sees a need to understand the many internal and external relationships necessary for the successful operation of an organization. He proposes structural responses to relationship problems. He also acknowledges the role that organizational culture and market preferences play in defining the competitive dynamics of an industry. He does not, however, provide a coherent model of the operation of relationships that can act as the basic unit of analysis for the chain of relationships.

Portfolio analysis analyzes the resource types of an organization and their characteristics. Product analysis classifies products into types such as cash cows, stars, dogs, problem children. These types identify the likely market profile of the products. Other similar analytical techniques provide understanding of the skills profile and structural components of organizations.

Traditionally structural analysis has focused on concepts such as hierarchies, matrix management, and levels of centralization. While these are elements of structure, they are also characteristic of relationships. These relationships are, however, determined not merely by structure but by the influences of all elements of the social and economic environment.

The lack of understanding about the complete set of relationships in organizations makes it difficult to develop considered and controlled responses to building organizational structures. The terms used in the analysis of the social environment of organizations often include:

- leadership
- management styles
- coalitions
- stakeholders
- power
- culture
- societal influences

These different concepts are used to provide structures to understand the social environment. The problem with this approach is the lack of a coherent model within which to place these different views and to understand their interactions. Further this social environment is not divorced from the business environment, its resources, and its organizational structures. Rather it is the system within which those elements operate. A more effective approach to understanding the influences of power, expectation, and change would enable all of these components to be analyzed within an overall integrated framework of social and economic action.

The Limitation of Current Approaches and the Contribution of Relationship Dynamics

The factors that influence the successful operation of organizations include economic, political, cultural, social, moral, and psychological factors. The traditional analytical techniques, identified above, do not have underlying models that can deal effectively with the nonfinancial factors.

Relationship Dynamics provides just such a model. The impact of all of these elements can be identified and analyzed using the relationship mechanism. Relationship Dynamics provides a technique for quickly capturing the relationships that are operating in a business environment and then evaluating them. The nature of much of this information is that it is not wholly deterministic. It is therefore not possible to take the data points alone and extrapolate or interpolate their meaning; it is also necessary to understand how the relationship mechanism operates and determines much of our social, moral, political, and cultural behavior. Further, relationships provide an external, observable basis for analysis, unlike those techniques that focus on the internal psychological elements of individuals.

Relationship Dynamics also provides an incisive first cut of the key operational issues that organizations will encounter. By providing an analysis process based on this complete framework of the interaction among entities in the business domain, strategic issues can be fully and powerfully evaluated.

Using Relationship Analysis for Strategic Analysis

Relationship Analysis provides a very effective first-stage analysis process for strategic analysis. The Relationship

Scoping and Relationship Alignment phases provide a fast and direct mechanism to generate an overall view of the operation of an organization. From this first level of analysis, detail issues can be evaluated through Relationship Profiling or other analytical techniques, such as process analysis, information analysis, and the more traditional strategic analysis approaches identified above.

A major strength of Relationship Analysis is its ability to provide a map of the key interactions an organization has, which can then be evaluated in terms of the most appropriate detailed elements. The high-level relationship map enables the key issues to be identified and any information gathered to be integrated back into a coherent model.

For example, the relative impact of employee, regulator, supplier, and customer relationships can be quickly evaluated for their impact on profitability. Specific issues of concern or opportunity can then be identified and investigated in relation to the contribution of the different relationships. The resulting information then provides an integrated view of the operation of the whole organization. This view enables the "softer" issues, based on emotion, control, and structure, to be evaluated within the same framework as the "harder" issues, based on product performance and financial return.

RELATIONSHIP MARKETING

The external relationships of an organization are determined by the nature of the transactions that the organization and its component entities enter into. External relationships can belong to a number of types. They include partnership, regulatory, and philanthropic-based relationships as well those based on the dynamic transaction roles of customer and supplier. In this section we will focus on market-based relationships, because the issues raised about them in this more naked environment also apply to the other types of relationships.

The analysis of a market positions an organization and its component entities as suppliers and customers. The classic approach to market analysis is based on Michael Porter's definition of markets and competition. This defines market relationships in terms of:

- customer behavior
- an organization's products in terms of cost leadership, differentiation, and focus
- an organization's internal structure in terms of generating added value
- an organization in relation to competitors
- the potential for development of a market, using concepts such as market maturity

Each of these aspects for analysis has traditionally been evaluated in terms of the economic exchange that occurs between organizations and individuals. The language of analysis is in terms of products, value, and substitution. This language is perfectly acceptable when the objects of market operation, products, and services are relatively static and mechanistic. This approach does not, however, capture many of the other important elements of external market operation.

For example, if the car market is seen as facilitating access to a mix of raw materials with a physical performance, a mechanistic approach is applicable. If, however, the car market is driven more by the intangible elements of the product and includes the interactions with the manufacturer and dealer, the mechanistic approach to market analysis begins to break down. Many cars are purchased on the basis of image and appearance, rather than simple product specification.

The traditional mechanistic approach becomes even more of a problem as the products being exchanged in the market become less physical and the more intangible, service and image-based products come to the fore. The value of such products varies wildly as customer perceptions and preferences change. Such changes cannot be identified as having a simple causal driver.

The existing approaches to market analysis provide much useful information. However, a more effective understanding is gained by the addition of Relationship Dynamics. Before analyzing the mechanistic change in a market, the surrounding relationship matrix needs to be taken into account. In order to enter the market a relationship must be built with suppliers and customers. This relationship can range from a transient one, which lasts for a few seconds as a simple exchange is made, to a lifetime relationship covering many exchanges. Additionally existing relationships will impact upon the likelihood of a customer or supplier forming new relationships.

The addition of Relationship Dynamics to the techniques used for analyzing the external market relationships of organizations and individuals enables a much more complete analysis to take place. It also provides a powerful high-level tool that can be used strategically to generate a fast and incisive understanding of the overall operation of the market.

SUGGESTIONS FOR
FURTHER READING

The concepts introduced in this book are based on many threads
of development and understanding. For those interested in extending their appreciation of how *Relationship Dynamics* can be
applied to specific situations, further reading can be found in
many books, some of which are listed below.

The Push for Relationship Management

Tom Peters has spent many years promoting the concepts of excellence and customer focus. In his latest books he has identified the
key role that relationships play in the sustainability of any organization and market. While he promotes the need to focus on the
quality of relationships, he also bemoans the lack of any systematic model of analysis that can be used to capture information
about relationships in operation. Readers interested in examining
many examples of specific situations in which the relationship dimension is crucial should read:

Peters, Tom. *Liberation Management, Necessary Disorganization for
the Nanosecond Nineties.* New York: Alfred A. Knopf, 1992.

Peters, Tom. *The Pursuit Of The Wow!* New York: Random House, 1994.

Relationship Marketing

There are a whole raft of books on the development of marketing into a concept called "Relationship Marketing." When analyzed in detail, this concept appears to provide much justification for considering the totality of relationships when attempting to understand behavior. However, few people have taken the concept any further and attempted to identify an underlying mechanism that can be directly investigated. Information that provides a good background to the issues behind "Relationship Marketing" can be found in:

Whiteley, Richard. *The Customer-Driven Company.* Reading, MA: Addison-Wesley, 1991.

Robinson, John Fraser. *Total Quality Marketing.* London: Kogan Page, 1991.

The Non-Deterministic Nature of Social Knowledge

A key concept in *Relationship Dynamics* is the notion that complex structures, particularly social structures, operate in a dimension of probabilistic as well as deterministic outcomes. Therefore we should not be looking to find a formula for understanding relationships; rather we should be searching for key patterns and effective learning outcomes that enable us to dynamically understand the world around us. This concept has long been held in the physical sciences and its relevance is well described by:

Bronowski, Jacob. *The Ascent of Man.* British Broadcasting Corporation, 1973.

Prigogine, Ilya, and Stengers, Isabelle. *Order Out Of Chaos— Man's New Dialogue With Nature.* New York: Harper Collins, 1985.

Examples of Relationship Focus In Industry

There have been many books written on the operation of companies that focus on the nature of management practice. Many general books have been written, such as those by Tom Peters and Rosabeth Moss Kantor, which are well worth reading. For a detailed study of the internal dynamics of a major organization, studies of IBM are most enlightening. IBM dominated the computer industry in the 1960s, 1970s, and 1980s. In the nineties, they are still the largest company in the computing industry, but are no longer the dominant force. Their last ten years have been a struggle to refashion the internal and external relationships upon which the organization is based. This struggle is well documented by:

Carroll, Paul. *Big Blues—The Unmaking of IBM.* New York: Crown Publishing, 1993.

The Move Beyond Quality

The quality movement has become relatively mature, with a well-defined approach to the analysis of industrial processes. As these processes have been extended to the more people-orientated areas of companies, they have provided a degree of control and rigor that was often previously missing. However, in promoting approaches based on the evaluation of large-scale repeatable processes with static machinery, they have somewhat missed the point. Social processes are based on a dynamic, ever-changing base of people who do not provide a consistent response to any given stimulus. As a result a new approach, based on the concept of a "system" rather than a "process," is being developed. These ideas have been explored by:

Flood, Robert L. *Beyond T.Q.M.* New York: John Wiley & Sons, 1993.

The Impact of Process Reengineering and the Need to Manage Change

Process reengineering is at a crossroads. The basic concept of reviewing the operation of an organization in order to generate more easily operated customer-focused processes is a sound one. However, process reengineering has gained a bad name because many firms and consultants have attempted to provide a quick fix under its umbrella. Fundamental change in organizations requires that careful thought and time be given to the impact on the individuals in the organization and their relationships. This step has often been left out. The initial gurus of process reengineering always identified this issue as a key one. For those readers interested in applying process reengineering effectively (assisted by the careful management of relationships), Hammer's and Champy's latest books provide excellent examples.

Hammer, Mike. *The Reengineering Revolution*. New York: Harper-Collins, 1995.

Champy, James. *Reengineering Management—The Mandate for New Leadership*. New York: HarperCollins, 1995.

INDEX

ABOUT THE AUTHORS

JAMES MUSGRAVE has a BSc, joint honors in Sociology and Social History. Through his firm, the Musgrave Partnerships, he provides long-term health care and corporate training in the latest analytical techniques that he has developed for the assessment of client case load and risk profiles. For CHC Consulting, his principal functions are the development and presentation of corporate training seminars that introduce and apply Relationship Dynamics for management solutions. He lives in Nairn, Scotland.

MICHAEL ANNISS has a BSc in Psychology and a Post Graduate Certificate in Education. He was formerly a Senior I.T. Consultant at AT&T Istel and Hewlett Packard. He now provides organizations, worldwide, with education, consulting, and transition services in both the implementation of leading edge computing technologies and relationship development and management. He lives in Nairn, Scotland.